PITA
THE GREAT

PITA
THE GREAT

BY VIRGINIA T. HABEEB

EBURY PRESS · LONDON

Published by Ebury Press
Division of the National Magazine Company Ltd
Colquhoun House
27-37 Broadwick Street
London W1V 1FR

Illustrations by Emanuel Schongut

First published by Workman Publishing Company Inc, New York

ISBN 0 85223 650 6

Computerset in Great Britain by MFK Typesetting Ltd, Hitchin, Herts.
Printed and bound in Great Britain at the University Press, Cambridge

DEDICATION

This book is dedicated with love to
my mother Rose, my dearest inspiration,
and my father, Mitchel, who could accept
nothing less than perfection, especially
in mother's pita bread. It was!

ACKNOWLEDGMENTS

Working with these recipes and refining those handed down from family to family has been a labour of love. And living with *Pita the Great*, even more! It has filled me with many warm memories of family and friends and it has opened up a world of understanding in the gastronomic differences that abound from region to region in the Middle East.

I feel about work as did the venerable Kahlil Gibran, who was a friend of my father during their early years together in America, and who said, "Work is love made visible. And if you cannot work with love, but only with distaste, it is better that you should leave your work and sit at the gate of the temple and take alms of those who work with joy."

My warmest thanks to my family and friends who have offered their suggestions and recipes and especially to:

• Mitchell Habeeb, my husband, whose critical taste and discerning palate would refine even the most perfect recipe.

• Suzanne Rafer who first saw the potential of combining the age-old tradition of baking pita with the first health foods of civilization and who has been a constant source of inspiration.

• My editor, Susan Gough Henly who conceived of blending the culinary heritage of the Middle East with the eclectic foods of today and who has made the book work so beautifully.

• Bob Gilbert, who tested the recipes, making certain we had refined our directions for your ease of understanding and preparation.

CONTENTS

PITA AND YOGURT

PICKER UPPERS

3
PITA ALONG-SIDES

4

PITA INSIDES

5

PITA SWEETS

A Word From The Author

Although I grew up in the wonderful and majestic hills of West Virginia, both my parents were Middle Eastern and I was steeped in their heritage. In my earliest childhood days I was introduced to the versatility and tasty goodness of pita, it being the centre of every family meal and party occasion.

Having always enjoyed the pleasures of pita—the same "miracle" loaves of Bible history that I learned about in Sunday school—I am not at all surprised that it has become the "in" bread of health-conscious America today.

In our home, my mother lovingly baked pita every week and delighted in serving it with all the delicious foods that showed it at its best—*hummus bi tahini*, *baba ghanouge*, and all sorts of delicious lamb concoctions such as *Kibbeh*, stuffed grape leaves, and yogurt soup with pita dumplings, to name a few.

Later on, when I travelled throughout the Middle East I explored the streets or "souks" of old Jerusalem and Cairo with their stalls laden with lamb, fish, olives, marrow, sesame seeds, pulses, tomatoes, nuts, figs, oranges, and lemons. I saw townspeople take their homemade pita dough to be baked in commercial ovens or *furh-ins* for the evening meal and watched delivery boys and old men carry mounds of baked pita to the street-side markets. And, I can still taste the sumptuous appetizers we sampled from elaborate *meze* trays in the courtyards of Caesaria.

Pita continues to play a central role in our everyday meals and when we entertain. My husband, Mitchell Habeeb, also of Middle-Eastern ancestry, makes all our own yogurt and yogurt cheese. He tells some exciting tales of his days as a U.S. Army officer in the Middle East. The most appealing to me are the stories of his early-morning breakfasts of pita, yogurt cheese, plump black olives, fresh cucumbers, and tomatoes, which have now become a staple for us.

In my professional career as a home economist and food editor I have been able to combine my love of pita-based recipes with an eclectic knowledge of, and fascination with, all types of food. I hope you will share my passion as you enjoy *Pita the Great*.

Virginia T. Habeeb
June, 1986

PITA THE GREAT

In ancient times it was believed to be the staff of life; today it is newly acknowledged as the tastiest and most versatile natural food: pita, the puffed little loaf with the pocket in the middle, comes to us from the very cradle of our civilization.

Stories tell of bedouins wandering the desert plains under the sweltering sun. When night fell and the temperature dropped they would pitch their tents and prepare the evening meal. Mixing a batch of powdered grain and water, they'd pat it into flat rounds and "bake" it over an open fire, probably atop the same vessel used to mix the dough. The milk that the bedouins carried in their sheepskin and goatskin bags would also, by night, have become a thick and tangy custard-like curd: the first yogurt and a perfect pita accompaniment.

From its traditional beginnings as the mainstay of simple nomad fare and exotic Middle

Eastern feasts, pita has made an amazing conquest of the European palate. Not only is it associated with the traditional *Shish Kebab* and other sublime Middle-Eastern classics like *Hummus Bi Tahini*, *Baba Ghanouge*, *Falafel*, *Kefta Kebabs*, *Kibeh*, and *Tabbouleh*. Now it scoops up Oriental and Black Bean Dip, Basil Fondue Piedmontese, and Chicken Liver Pâté; is a pocketful of seafood, chicken, vegetable, fruit, and nut salads; is transformed into tarts, triangles, croûtons, pyramids, crêpes, and pies; and can even be dropped into soups as dumplings.

Pita is known by many names depending upon its country or region of origin. And, also depending upon the recipe itself and the way it is handled or baked, it may or may not have a pocket in the middle. In Greece it is called *pita* and is usually pocketless, *pide* in Turkey, *kemaj* in Lebanon, *aysh* in Egypt, *khubiz* in Syria and Morocco, *kesra* in Algeria. In Britain we've adopted the Greek term *pita* even though our bread has a pocket.

Whatever its origin and name, pita is a lightly leavened round loaf (measuring anywhere from five to nine inches) with a soft crust and generally a hollow centre. Usually made without shortening or milk, it is baked in a very hot oven for only a few minutes. It puffs quickly as it bakes but falls slightly when it is removed from the oven and cools. Hence, its famous pocket, the Pandora's box for creative cooks everywhere.

Some versions are made

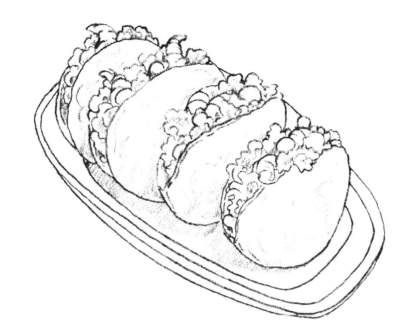

Pita is appealing because it is healthy, convenient, and versatile. You can split it, tear it or roll it, you can fill it, wrap it, dip it, top it; you can bake it, fry it, and toast it; you can make it and buy it.

Low in sodium, fat, and calories, pita is most often matched with yogurt, olives, cucumbers, tomatoes, bulgur, chickpeas, aubergines, sesame seeds, nuts, and the natural sweeteners: dates, apricots, oranges, pomegranates, and quince—foods born of the earliest civilizations. Given our current fascination with this chewy, flavourful bread, we are now enjoying the world's first health foods in new and creative combinations.

Let this book be your inspiration as it draws on the age-old culinary traditions of the Middle East and then takes off with a cornucopia of enticing new recipes that throw open all the marvellous possibilities that pita presents.

without any leavening and are baked on top of the range on a concave pan. The Lebanese *marook* is shaped by hand in much the same manner as pizza, by tossing and stretching the dough until it is well over a foot in size. It is then flipped on to a concave-shaped metal surface set over a heat source where it bakes quickly in minutes. The Armenians have a similar bread, called *lavash*, which is baked to a cracker-like crispness and measures anywhere from five to twenty inches.

ABOUT THE RECIPES

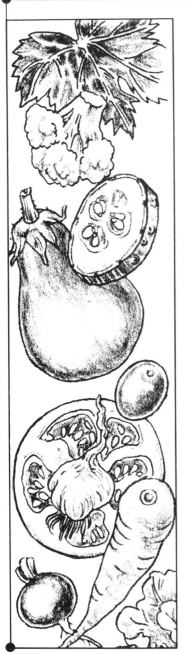

- Recipes throughout are interchangeable as pita go-withs. Many of the appetizers may be used for sandwiches. Salad and sandwich fillings may be served as appetizers. All may be extended into full-course meals with some creative imagination.
- Throughout *Pita The Great*, I've suggested a specific kind of pita for each recipe. You can, of course, substitute your favourite pita variation for what is listed. It is an accommodating bread for an uncommonly limitless variety of uses.
- All yields are approximate. Creative cooks may shrink or stretch ingredients at will as they adjust recipes to include more, less, or additional ingredients. I have indicated yields for salad sandwiches, dips and spreads by approximate weight rather than number of servings. Depending on what other dishes you are offering and how large your pitas are, you can then decide how much you want to serve each person.
- Where appropriate, Middle Eastern names are given along with the English recipe titles. A brief explanation of the Middle Eastern name and origin is also included.
- With all Middle Eastern and Mediterranean recipes, seasonings and proportions for similar classic recipes will vary from region to region in the countries of their origin. Keep in mind that these recipes are general guidelines. I have given you fairly basic proportions for each recipe which you can adjust and experiment with according to your personal taste. This is best described as *"the-more-or-less-principle."* Take for example *Hummus Bi Tahini*, page 40. If you like a tart flavour, use *more* lemon juice. If you are a garlic

devotee, use *twice* as much. This is creative cookery at its best. Be adventuresome!

• The abundant use of herbs and spices in the recipes enhances the flavour of pita. Such piquantly seasoned dishes lend themselves to the elimination or reduction of salt for a healthier diet.

• Most Middle Eastern meat recipes call for lamb—however, its beef or veal counterpart is acceptable. Those who are on special diets may substitute minced chicken for minced lamb or beef with the exception of Bulgur and Lamb Tartare, page 53. In recipes where lamb only is mentioned, it is preferable.

• Butter is lightly salted unless otherwise noted. For clarified butter, see page 56.

• On grilled meat and seafood *kebabs* I've given you general guidelines on distances away from the heat but it is wise to follow the directions for the particular cooker you are using.

• A blender or food processor is a must. Many of the recipes call for chopped, minced, diced, mashed, or puréed ingredients and these appliances shortcut such tedious tasks.

PITA AND YOGURT

Contained in this chapter are my tried and true secrets to baking perfect pita every time. Before you start, read the general tips and individual recipes carefully and you're sure to be rewarded with light, chewy pitas complete with drip-free pockets. And, once you've made your own pitas, you'll be hooked forever and won't think twice about whipping up a batch of Herbed Zahter Pita to go with Herb-Grilled Chicken and Onion, or Griddle-Baked Pita (the easiest of all) for Pita Cheese Crêpes with Orange-Blossom Syrup. In addition, I show you how to make pita toast, croûtons, and crisps.

Also in this chapter are our family recipes for yogurt, yogurt cheese, and white cheese—classic pita accompaniments in the Middle-East and now popular as part of the European diet in this health-conscious age. While a yogurt-making appliance is handy, my recipe shows you how to make yogurt on your cooker with a minimum of fuss. All these products are good sources of calcium, riboflavin, and protein and contain none of the fillers and preservatives that are so common in many commercial variations.

SECRETS TO BAKING PERFECT PITA

Rolling and Baking

• Handle the dough carefully. Reserve enough of a draft-free work surface to place as many rolled pitas as 24 small or 12 large.

• The key to rolling a smooth, well-rounded pita loaf is to roll from the centre of each ball of dough, giving the dough a ¼ turn after each roll. Carefully flip the circles over to smooth out any creases that might prevent a pocket from forming.

• As you roll each ball, cover the remaining balls with towels that you have sprinkled very lightly with warm water to keep the surface of the dough supple and moist.

• It will take approximately 30 minutes to roll out 24 small pitas. By the time you have rolled the last pita, begin baking the first ones you have rolled which have then risen for 30 minutes. Remember to preheat the oven and baking sheet 15 minutes before the pitas have finished rising.

• A very hot oven is a must. Make certain the oven has returned to temperature before baking each batch and don't keep opening the oven to check on the pitas while they are baking. The high heat makes the dough rise and puff literally in seconds. The bread bakes quickly, in minutes, and browns lightly on the bottom. If you want a more golden top, flip small pitas over after 4 minutes, large ones after 3 to 3½ minutes and bake up to 1 minute longer; be careful not to let the loaves get crisp and brittle.

• Pita bakes and puffs best on a preheated baking sheet placed on the bottom rack of the oven. Bake 1 sheet at a time for best results. For pitas that don't puff (Herbed Zahter Pita and

Sweetened Sesame Pita) you may bake 2 sheets at once. Add a second rack in the oven close to the first rack. Place 1 sheet on each rack, staggering 1 on the right and 1 on the left, and reverse the sheets from the top to bottom racks halfway through baking for even heat distribution.

• Whatever you do, remember practice makes perfect!

Cutting

• To make a single sandwich pocket, cut off the top of the pita leaving just enough space to gain access to the inside easily.

• To make 2 pocket sandwiches, cut a medium or large pita in half.

• To make 2 pancakes or rounds (for use as bases for tarts or wraps for fillings), slit a pita completely around.

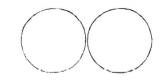

• To make small wedges for appetizers, cut a medium pita into 6 triangles; to make larger wedges for sandwich snacks, cut a larger pita into 6 or 8 triangles.

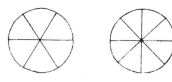

Storage and Thawing

• Wrap baked pitas immediately as they come from the oven in clean, dry cotton tea-towels (keep plenty on hand) until they are cool enough to handle. Then remove the warm pitas from the towels and place them in plastic bags. The insides of the bags will develop a slight moisture condensation as the loaves cool, which will keep them soft. Let the loaves cool completely before sealing the bags and storing.

● Store pita in plastic bags in the refrigerator for up to 1 week or in the freezer for up to 3 months.

● To thaw, let the frozen loaves stand, covered, at room temperature for 15 to 20 minutes.

● To heat, if desired, wrap in kitchen foil and place in a preheated oven at 150°C (300°F) mark 2 until warm and softened, 1 to 2 minutes. Do not overheat or the crust will become dry and brittle.

Buying Pita

Once available only in speciality bakeries and gourmet delis, pita is now found in most supermarkets. Commercially baked pitas tend to be made of either white flour or wholemeal flour and come in the following sizes:

Small: about 12.5 cm
    (5 inches) round
Medium: about 12.5×20.5 cm
    (5×8 inches oval)
Large: about 19 cm (7½ inches)
    round

BASIC PITA

Contrary to the standard method of allowing bread dough to rise before shaping, these loaves are *first* shaped and rolled, then allowed to rise before baking. This simplified version, which cuts preparation time by about 1½ to 2 hours, lets the yeast do its best work in the oven, thus assuring a better pocket. The result—a superior pita with a delightfully chewy, yet tender texture and a puff in every loaf!

475 ml (16 fl oz) warm water
15 g (½ oz) dried yeast
2.5 ml (½ tsp) sugar
10 ml (2 tsp) salt
700–800 g (1½–1¾ lb) strong white
  flour, plus flour for kneading

1.   Pour the water into a large bowl and sprinkle in the yeast. Stir to dissolve.

2.   With a wooden spoon, stir the sugar and salt into the yeast mixture; mix thoroughly. Gradually add 700 g (1½ lb) of the flour, stirring constantly until the dough is smooth. Slowly work in the remaining flour (up to 100 g (4 oz) with your hands, kneading until the dough is no longer sticky. Turn the dough out on to a well-floured board. Knead until it is smooth and elastic, about 5 minutes.

3.   Shape the dough into an even rectangle and cut it in half lengthwise. Divide the dough into 24 portions for small pitas; 12 for larger ones. Shape each portion into a smooth ball. Place the balls on a floured surface and cover them with slightly damp tea-towels while you roll out 1 ball at a time.

4.   Gently press each ball flat with your fingers, keeping it well rounded. Flour a work surface and a rolling pin.

Roll each round from the centre to the outer edge, giving the dough a ¼ turn after each roll, to form a perfect circle not quite 0.5 cm (¼ inch) thick (12.5–13.5 cm (5–5½ inches) in diameter for small pitas; 21.5 cm (8½ inches) for larger ones). Carefully flip the circles over to smooth out any creases that might prevent the pocket from forming.

5.   Fifteen minutes before the loaves have finished rising, preheat the oven to 240°C (475°F) mark 9. At the same time, place an ungreased baking sheet in the oven.

6.   As each loaf is rolled, place it carefully on a floured surface and cover with a clean dry tea-towel; do not let the surface of the loaves dry out. Let the loaves rise in a warm draught-free area, 30 to 45 minutes.

7.   To bake, place 4 small pitas or 1 large pita on the hot baking sheet. Bake on the bottom rack of the oven until puffed and lightly browned on the bottom and almost white on top, about 4 minutes for small pitas and 3½ minutes for large; the pita will be soft and flexible. If desired, flip the loaves over after they have puffed and bake up to 1 minute longer to brown the tops; be careful not to let the pita get crisp and brittle.

8.   Remove the hot pitas from the oven and wrap immediately in clean, dry tea-towels until cool enough to handle. Serve warm or at room temperature. For information on storage and thawing, see page 19.

9.   Repeat this process until all the pitas are baked.

Makes 24 small or 12 large pitas.

Variation *Poppy-Seed or Sesame Pita:*   After rolling out each circle of dough in step 4, brush the tops lightly with water and sprinkle with poppy seeds or toasted sesame seeds, page 165. Let the loaves rise and bake as above.

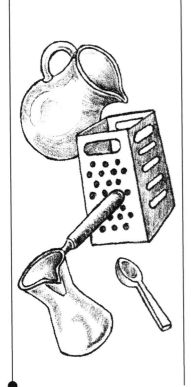

PITA CROÛTONS

B e cook-wise and penny smart! Save all those tops you cut off pitas that you fill. Make plain, cheese, or garlic croûtons. They're wonderful in salads and especially good on top of a bowl of soup!

250 g (9 oz) pita scraps, cut in 2.5–4 cm (1–1½ inch) pieces
50 g (2 oz) butter
60 ml (4 tbsp) olive oil

1.   Preheat the oven to 190°C (375°F) mark 5.

2.   Melt the butter in the oil in a small saucepan over medium heat.

3.   Spread the pita pieces in a baking pan. Pour the melted butter and oil over the top and toss gently to coat.

4.   Bake in the oven, stirring occasionally, until lightly browned and crisp, about 15 to 20 minutes.

Makes 250 g (9 oz).

Variations *Garlic Croûtons:*   Add 1 to 2 cloves of crushed garlic to the melted butter and oil.
Cheese Croûtons: Sprinkle plain or garlic croûtons with grated Parmesan cheese when you remove them from the oven and toss to coat evenly.
   To store, refrigerate in an airtight container for up to 1 month or freeze for up to 3 months.

WHOLEMEAL HONEY PITA

This recipe contains a mixture of wholemeal and strong white flour to create a nutty-flavoured pita. Wholemeal flour is made from the ground kernels of whole wheat and contains all the bran and the wheat germ, as well as the starchy endosperm. The high gluten content of the strong white flour in combination with the wholemeal flour helps to increase the dough's elasticity. This enables it to retain the bubbles of gas from the yeast, allowing it to rise or "grow" to its fullest and form a large pocket. Because wheat germ contains oil, wholemeal flour will go rancid; if you don't use it very often, store it in the freezer.

350 g (12 oz) wholemeal flour
450 g (1 lb) strong white flour, plus flour for kneading
475 ml (16 fl oz) warm water
15 g (½ oz) dried yeast
15 ml (1 tbsp) honey
5 ml (1 tsp) salt

1. Combine the wholemeal and white flours in a large bowl; mix thoroughly. Set aside.

2. Pour the water into a second large bowl and sprinkle in the yeast. Stir to dissolve.

3. With a wooden spoon, stir the honey and salt into the yeast mixture; mix thoroughly. Gradually add 700 g (1½ lb) of the flour, stirring constantly, until the dough is smooth. Slowly work in the remaining flour (up to 100 g (4 oz)) with your hands, kneading until the dough is no longer sticky. Turn the dough out onto a well-floured board. Knead until it is smooth and elastic, about 5 minutes.

4. Shape the dough into an even rectangle and cut it in half lengthwise. Divide the dough into 24 portions for small pitas; 12 for larger ones. Shape each portion into a smooth ball. Place the balls on a floured surface and cover them with slightly damp tea-towels while you roll out 1 ball at a time.

5. Gently press each ball flat with your fingers, keeping it well rounded. Flour a work surface and rolling pin. Roll each round from the centre to the outer edge, giving the dough a ¼ turn after each roll, to form a perfect circle not quite 0.5 cm (¼ inch) thick (about 12.5–13.5 cm (5–5½ inches) for small pitas; about 21.5 cm (8½ inches) for larger ones). Carefully flip the circles over to smooth out any creases that might prevent the pocket from forming.

6. As each loaf is rolled, place it carefully on a floured surface and cover with a clean, dry tea-towel; do not let the surface of the loaves dry out. Let the loaves rise in a warm, draft-free area, 30 to 50 minutes.

7. Fifteen minutes before the loaves have finished rising, preheat the oven to 240°C (475°F) mark 9. At the same time, place an ungreased baking sheet in the oven.

8. To bake, place 4 small pitas or 1 large pita on the hot baking sheet. Bake on the bottom rack of the oven until puffed and lightly browned on the bottom, about 4 minutes for small pitas and about 3½ minutes for large; the pita will be soft and flexible. If desired, flip the loaves over after they have puffed and bake up to 1 minute

longer to brown the tops; be careful not to let the pita get crisp and brittle.

9.   Remove the hot pitas from the oven and wrap immediately in clean, dry tea-towels until cool enough to handle. Serve warm or at room temperature. For information on storage and thawing, see page 19.

10.   Repeat this process until all the pitas are baked.

Makes 24 small or 12 large pitas.

Variations *Wholemeal Poppy-Seed or Sesame Pita:* After rolling out each circle of dough in Step 5, brush the tops lightly with water and sprinkle with poppy seeds or toasted sesame seeds, page 165. Let the loaves rise and bake as above.

Wheat Germ Honey Pita: Wheat germ, the heart of the wheat kernel which is the part of the whole grain removed in the milling of white flour, imparts a grainy, nutty-flavoured texture to pita. Remember to store wheat germ in the refrigerator once the package is opened.

50 g (2 oz) wheat germ
700 g (1½ lb) strong white flour
475 ml (16 fl oz) warm water
15 g (½ oz) dried yeast
15 ml (1 tbsp) honey
5 ml (1 tsp) salt

1.   Combine the wheat germ and flour in a large bowl; mix thoroughly. Set aside.

2.   Follow the directions from Step 2 of Wholemeal Honey Pita above.

Makes 24 small or 12 large pitas.

WHAT TO DO WITH PITAS IF THEY DON'T PUFF

Check the Secrets to Baking Perfect Pita, page 18; perhaps the oven or the baking sheet is not as hot as it should be; perhaps there is a crease or a crack in the dough? No matter how perfect the dough or the technique, sometimes you'll find an occasional pita that will not puff as much as it should. Whatever you do, don't throw it away. Here are some clever uses for these errant loaves:

Make Breadsticks or Crisps   Preheat the oven to 200°C (400°F) mark 6. Cut the pitas into strips and spread them with softened butter. Roll them in snipped chives, finely chopped nuts, poppy, caraway, or sesame seeds, or grated Parmesan cheese. Place on a baking sheet and bake until bubbly, 5 to 10 minutes. If you want crispy sticks, bake them longer. Make savoury or sweet triangles using the seasonings for Pita Crisps, page 28.

Make Garlic Toast   Spread with softened butter seasoned with crushed garlic and grill until lightly browned and bubbly.

Make Plain, Cheese, or Garlic Croûtons   Cut into 2.5 cm (1 inch) pieces and prepare croûtons, page 22.

Make Bread Crumbs   Preheat the oven to 240°C (475°F) mark 6. Tear the pitas into pieces, place them on a baking sheet, and bake until they are crisp and dry, but not browned. Or dry them at room temperature for several days until they are crisp. Place the crispy pieces in a blender or food processor fitted with the metal blade and process until fine and crumbly. Or place them in a paper bag and roll with a rolling pin until crumbly. To store, refrigerate in an airtight container for up to 1 month.

Make Pizzas   Toast one side until lightly browned. Turn the pita over and top with tomato sauce seasoned with oregano, garlic, and olive oil. Add a choice of your favourite ingredients such as mushrooms, pepperoni, green pepper, and onion. Sprinkle with grated mozzarella cheese and grill until hot and bubbly.

Make Bread Pudding   Cut into 5 cm (1½ inch) pieces and make Spiced Apple Pita Pudding with Vanilla Sauce, page 153.

Make Pocket Bread Salad   Tear pita into pieces and make Pocket Bread salad (Fattoush), page 101.

Make Quick Zahter or Herbed Bread   Drizzle the loaves with olive oil, sprinkle with zahter, page 166, or another favourite herb, and grill until hot and bubbly, 1 to 2 minutes.

HERBED ZAHTER PITA

Zahter is a piquant blend of herbs including thyme, marjoram, toasted sesame seeds, and sumac, the tart dried seeds of the sumac plant. To make an acceptable substitute, see the recipe on page 166. The tantalizing aroma of Zahter Pita in the oven is enough to break the resolutions of even the most serious dieter! Just as with Sweetened Sesame Pita, Herbed Zahter Pita does not puff because the herb mixture has been pressed into the dough.

1 recipe Basic Pita, page 21,
*   prepared up to step 2*
25 g (1 oz) zahter (see page 166)
175 ml (6 fl oz) olive oil

1. Shape the dough into an even rectangle and cut it in half lengthwise. Divide the dough into 12 portions. Shape each portion into a smooth ball. Place the balls on a floured surface and cover them with slightly damp tea-towels to keep the surface of the dough supple and moist. Let the balls rise in a warm, draught-free place for 30 to 45 minutes.

2. Fifteen minutes before the loaves have finished rising, preheat the oven to 220°C (425°F) mark 7. Lightly grease a baking sheet.

3. Blend the zahter and the olive oil in a small bowl to make a thin paste. Set aside.

4. Working on 2 balls at a time and using your fingertips, gently press 2 balls flat, keeping them well rounded. Flour a work surface and rolling pin. Roll each round from the centre to the outer edge to form an 18 cm (7 inch) circle.

5. Place the 2 rounds on the baking sheet. Spread the zahter paste evenly over the top of each round (15 ml (1 tbsp) per round) pressing down with your fingertips to make the mixture stick.

6. Bake until the loaves are golden-brown and the seeds are toasted, 10 to 12 minutes. The bread should be soft not crisp. It will bake best if you bake 1 sheet at a time on an oven rack placed in the centre or lower third of your oven. However, since this bread does not puff, if you wish to bake 2 sheets at a time, add another rack in the oven close to the first rack. Place 1 sheet on each rack, staggering 1 on the right and 1 on the left, and reverse the sheets from the top to bottom racks half-way through baking for even heat distribution.

7. Transfer to wire racks and let stand until cool enough to handle. Cut into wedges and serve warm or at room temperature. For information on storage and thawing, see page 19.

8. Repeat with the remaining dough, baking one batch before rolling and preparing the next.

Makes 12 loaves or 96 triangles.

SPICED ANISEED TEA
(Shī Yensoon)

This exotic blend of spices join together to make a warm and tingly tea, perfect for a cold winter's afternoon or eve. Serve it with Pita Tea Sandwiches, page 49, or with Sweet Sesame Crisps, cheese, and fruit slices. On a hot day, offer it iced, topped with lemon slices and chopped walnuts.

1.1 litres (2 pints) water
3 cinnamon sticks, broken in half
3 to 4 whole cloves
5 cm (2 inch) fresh ginger, peeled and chopped
10 ml (2 tsp) aniseeds
Sugar or honey, to taste
Chopped walnuts (garnish)

Pour the water into a large saucepan and add the cinnamon, cloves, ginger, and aniseeds. Bring to a boil. Reduce the heat and simmer until the water tastes of the spices and turns brown from their colour, 8 to 10 minutes. Stir in the sugar or honey to taste, or pass separately for optional use. Strain into teacups or glasses. Garnish each cup with a sprinkling of chopped walnuts.

Makes about 6 to 8 servings.

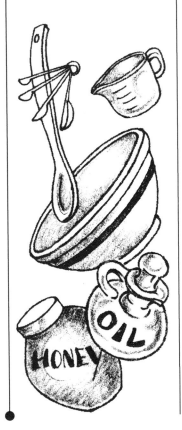

PITA TOAST

Pita makes heavenly toast. It's crisp and easy to handle.

Plain Toast: Split pitas into 2 rounds and toast (insides up) under the grill. Use in place of melba toast.

Buttered Toast: Split pitas into 2 rounds and spread the insides with softened butter. Toast under the grill until lightly browned. Serve with dips and pâtés or with smoked salmon or caviar.

PITA CRISPS

These fabulous crisps, adapted from a recipe of my good friend Delphine Wein of Boston, Massachusetts, are seasoned first then cut in wedges and baked to a light and crunchy crisp. I've created both savoury and sweet varieties to be used in myriad ways.

SWEET CRISPS

Cinnamon Crisps: Preheat the oven to 170°C (325°F) mark 3. Split pitas into 2 rounds and spread the insides with softened butter. Sprinkle with cinnamon and brown sugar. Cut into wedges and place on a baking sheet. Bake until crisp and lightly browned, about 10 to 15 minutes.

Sesame Crisps: Substitute sesame seeds for the cinnamon and follow the directions above.

SAVOURY CRISPS

Preheat the oven to 170°C (325°F) mark 3. Split pitas into 2 rounds and spread the insides with a mixture of softened butter and crushed garlic. Top with a choice of Parmesan cheese, poppy seeds, sesame seeds, oregano, or any other of your favourite seasonings.

Cut into wedges and place on a baking sheet. Bake until browned, about 10 to 15 minutes.

To store any of the above, cool and place in an airtight container. Refrigerate for up to 1 week or freeze for up to 3 months.

SWEETENED-SESAME PITA

Because you press sesame seeds into the dough in this recipe, these rounds will be flat, without the traditional pocket in the middle. The resulting pita have a delightfully chewy texture and sweet nutty flavour. Try them for dessert with fruit and cheese. They're guaranteed to bring raves when served with a glass of champagne.

1 recipe Basic Pita, page 21,
  prepared up to step 2
150 g (5 oz) sugar
60–90 ml (4–6 tbsp) cold water
175 g (6 oz) sesame seeds

1. Shape the dough into an even rectangle and cut it in half lengthwise. Divide the dough into 12 portions. Shape each portion into a smooth ball. Place the balls on a floured surface and cover them with slightly damp tea-towels to keep the surface of the dough supple and moist. Let the balls rest in a warm draught-free place 30 to 45 minutes.

2. Fifteen minutes before the loaves have finished rising, preheat the oven to 220°C (425°F) mark 7. Lightly grease a baking sheet.

3. Blend the sugar with 60 ml (4 tbsp) cold water in a small bowl to form a thick paste. Add up to 90 ml (6 tbsp) of water if necessary. Set aside.

4. Working on 2 balls at a time and using your fingertips, gently press each ball flat, keeping it well rounded. Flour a work surface and rolling pin. Roll out each round from the centre to the outer edge to form an 18 cm (7 inch) circle.

5. Place the 2 rounds on the baking sheet. Spread the sugar paste evenly over the top of each round with your fingertips. Sprinkle each round with 20 ml (4 tsp) of sesame seeds, spreading them to the edges of the dough to coat evenly. Press down with your fingertips to make the seeds stick. Score each circle into 8 wedges, cutting completely through but leaving the wedges in place.

6. Bake until the loaves are golden-brown and the seeds are toasted, 10 to 12 minutes. The bread should be soft not crisp. The bread will bake best if you bake one sheet at a time on an oven rack placed in the centre or lower third of your oven. However, since this bread does not puff, if you wish to bake 2 sheets at a time, add another rack in the oven close to the first rack. Place 1 sheet on each rack, staggering 1 on the right and 1 on the left, and reverse the sheets from the top to bottom racks halfway through baking for even heat distribution.

7. Separate the wedges and transfer to wire racks. Let stand until cool enough to handle.

8. Repeat with the remaining dough, baking one batch before rolling and preparing the next.

Makes 12 loaves or 96 triangles.

GRIDDLE-BAKED PITA PINWHEEL SANDWICHES

Spread each pita with softened butter then with the chosen filling. Depending on the size of the wheel desired, stack anywhere from 2 to 4 rounds on top of each other. Roll up like a Swiss roll. Seal the roll with softened butter then wrap it tightly with kitchen foil or cling film. Refrigerate to chill, at least 1 hour. Cut into 0.5 cm (¼ inch) slices. Try any of the following fillings.

SAVOURY
• Plain unsalted Yogurt Cheese, page 33, topped with thin slices of prosciutto. Place a thin pickled gherkin at one end of the top layer and roll from that end.
• Yogurt Cheese Spread mixed with chopped pimiento-stuffed olives, page 34.
• Gingered Fig Montrachet, page 71, topped with thin slices of cured ham.
• Yogurt Cheese Spread, mixed with finely chopped raw mushrooms, page 34, and topped with thinly sliced roast beef.
• Plain unsalted Yogurt Cheese, page 33, with thinly sliced smoked salmon topped with finely chopped capers. Place a marinated asparagus spear at one end of the top layer and roll from that end.
• Bulgur and Lamb Tartare, page 53, topped with finely chopped spring onions and toasted pine nuts.

SWEET
• Plain unsalted Yogurt Cheese, page 33, topped with a layer of finely chopped Spiced Glazed Figs, page 150.
• Plain unsalted Yogurt Cheese, page 33, sprinkled with cinnamon and brown sugar.
• Plain unsalted Yogurt Cheese, page 33, blended with crumbled halvah.
• Yogurt Cheese Spread mixed with raspberries or strawberries, page 34.

UNLEAVENED GRIDDLE-BAKED PITA

Wonderfully chewy and soft, this bread has no leavening agent and is "baked" on top of the cooker on a large griddle or frying pan. Griddle-Baked Pita probably most resemble the first ancient loaves desert nomads baked for their supper. Use them to wrap around kebabs or to make dessert crêpes.

450 g (1 lb) strong white flour or 275 g (10 oz) strong white flour and 175 g (6 oz) wholemeal flour, plus flour for kneading
5 ml (1 tsp) salt
225–350 ml (8–12 fl oz) warm water
Vegetable oil

1. Combine the flour and salt in a large bowl. Stirring with a wooden spoon, add enough water so the dough pulls away from the sides of the bowl and is no longer sticky; stir until smooth.

2. Turn out on to a well-floured board and knead until the dough is smooth and elastic, 5 minutes.

3. Shape the dough into an even rectangle and cut in half lengthwise. Divide the dough into 12 portions and shape into smooth balls. Cover with slightly damp tea-towels and let rest about 5 to 10 minutes.

4. Gently press each ball flat with your fingers, keeping it well rounded. Flour a work surface and rolling pin. Roll out each round to form a 15–18 cm (6–7 inch) circle, or until almost paper thin. Cover each round with a slightly damp tea-towel.

5. Lightly oil a griddle or large skillet and warm over medium-high heat until hot. Gently stretch each round as thin as possible without tearing as you place it on the griddle. Cook until browned, bubbly spots appear on the bottom, about 1½ minutes; turn and brown the other side. Remove from the griddle and immediately wrap in a clean tea-towel until cool enough to handle. Serve warm or at room temperature. For information on storage and thawing, see page 19.

6. Repeat with the remaining dough until all the pitas are cooked. Lightly oil the griddle after cooking 3 or 4 loaves; do not add too much oil or the pitas will be soggy and heavy.

Makes 12 pitas.

HOMEMADE YOGURT
(Laban)

Yogurt, or *Laban* as it is called in Syria and Lebanon, is a staple in our household to enjoy as is, to use as an ingredient in many special dishes, or to make *Labani*, a fresh yogurt cheese. This is my husband Mitch's recipe, tried and tested to a creamy delight and low-calorie to boot, if you make it with semi-skimmed milk. Skimmed milk powder helps to add richness and body without adding fat.

25 g (1 oz) low-fat milk powder
900 ml (1½ pints) pasteurised or
    semi-skimmed milk
60 ml (4 tbsp) natural yogurt starter
    (see note page 33)

1.   Combine the milk powder and whole milk in a large saucepan. Stir until dissolved.

2.   Heat the milk mixture over medium heat to 82°C (180°F) or until bubbles begin to appear around the edges and a skin forms on top. Stir the skin into the mixture.

3.   Remove from the heat and let cool to 49°C (120°F) or until the milk feels comfortably warm to your little finger or when dropped on your wrist.

4.   Put the yogurt starter in a small bowl and stir in about 100 ml (4 fl oz) of the lukewarm milk until the starter is completely dissolved. Add the yogurt mixture to the remaining luke-warm milk, stirring gently to blend.

5.   Pour into individual glass containers or a bowl. Cover with a clean, dry tea-towel and leave in a warm place, undisturbed until the yogurt is set, about 6 to 8 hours. The lower the percentage of fat in the milk, the longer the yogurt will take to set.

And, the longer it sets, the more tart the yogurt.

6.   To store, refrigerate, covered, for up to 1 week.

Makes 900 ml (1½ pints).

Secrets to Making Perfect Yogurt

● All utensils used in making and storing yogurt must be sterile.
● It is essential to use only pasteurised or semi-skimmed milk.
● Check the temperature with a thermometer. In the days before our modern technology, testing the temperature was "by guess and by gosh," but it also works very well. If you can dip your little finger into the warm milk and count slowly to 10 without burning your finger the milk is ready.

Note: For your first batch of homemade yogurt, use natural commerical yogurt (use one that has not been pasteurised) as your starter. From then on, save at least 60 ml (4 tbsp) from your last batch as the starter for your next. In the Middle East, they call this starter *rowbie*. In homes where large quantities of yogurt are made and consumed, it is possible that it could be a direct descendant from the last generation, from a grandmother, an aunt, or possibly a neighbour.

FRESH YOGURT CHEESE
(Labani)

This famous Middle Eastern cheese, called *Labani* (which means drained yogurt), has a delightfully piquant flavour and creamy texture. It is most often served for breakfast or as an appetizer with fresh pita. By adding different ingredients, yogurt cheese becomes a sweet or savoury delicacy. Our favourite way of eating *Labani* is for breakfast, drizzled with olive oil, sprinkled with mint, and served with sliced tomatoes, cucumbers, and Calamata olives.

5 ml (1 tsp) salt, or more to taste
1.7 litres (3 pints) natural yogurt, preferably homemade, page 32

1.   At least one day before serving, gently stir the salt into the yogurt.

2.   Line a colander with 4 single layers of cheesecloth. Pour the yogurt into the cheesecloth. Gather the corners into a bag and tie them together securely with a cord. Hang the bag over the kitchen tap high enough to drain into the sink, or suspend over a deep bowl. (You may leave the yogurt to drain in the colander, however suspending it allows a better drain and results in a firmer, more creamy curd.) Let it drain overnight or until the yogurt curd is firm. The texture should be the consistency of softened cream cheese.

3.   Remove from the bag and place in a container. To store, refrigerate, covered, for up to 1 week.

Makes about 900 ml (1½ pints)—low-fat yogurt, because of its high water content, will yield a little less, about 600 ml (1 pint).

Making Yogurt Cheese in a Commercial Container

Buy 900 ml (1½ pints) of commercial yogurt and stir in 2.5 ml (½ tsp) salt. Pierce the bottom of the container in several places with a sharp fork. Place the container in a colander and let the yogurt drain until all the whey is removed and the curd in the container is firm and spreadable. Season as desired. Refrigerate, covered, for up to 1 week.

Savoury Variations
Yogurt Cheese Spread:
1. In a medium bowl, season Yogurt Cheese, to taste, with crushed garlic; finely chopped pimiento-stuffed olives, raw mushrooms, or marinated sun-dried tomatoes; or chopped herbs such as basil, dill, parsley, or mint. Blend gently until smooth. Depress the top of the cheese in several places with the back of a spoon. Refrigerate, covered, until firm, at least 30 minutes.

2. Drizzle with olive oil and serve as an appetizer spread surrounded with Basic Pita, page 21, cut into wedges.

Yogurt Cheese Balls or Logs:
1. Divide the prepared cheese into 2 large or 12 small portions.

2. Place each portion on a double fold of cheesecloth and shape into a ball or log. Refrigerate, covered, until firm, at least 30 minutes.

3. Remove the cheesecloth and roll in any of the following: finely chopped parsley, freshly ground black pepper, finely chopped fresh mint, or crumbled dried mint. Drizzle with olive oil and serve with Herbed Zahter Pita, page 26, cut into wedges.

Sweet Variations
Yogurt Cheese Spread:
1. Omit the salt when making Yogurt Cheese.

2. Place the cheese in a medium bowl and add finely chopped raisins, dates, raspberries, or strawberries, to taste. Blend gently until smooth. Refrigerate, covered, until firm, at least 30 minutes. Serve as a breakfast spread or a dessert-cheese spread with Pita Toast, page 28.

Yogurt Cheese Balls or Logs:

1. Divide the unsalted cheese into balls or logs as directed in Savoury Yogurt Cheese, above. Refrigerate, covered, until firm, at least 30 minutes.

2. Remove the cheesecloth and roll in any of the following: finely chopped peanuts, finely chopped raisins, or a cinnamon-sugar blend.

3. Serve as a brunch confection or for afternoon tea with Sweet Sesame Crisps, page 28.

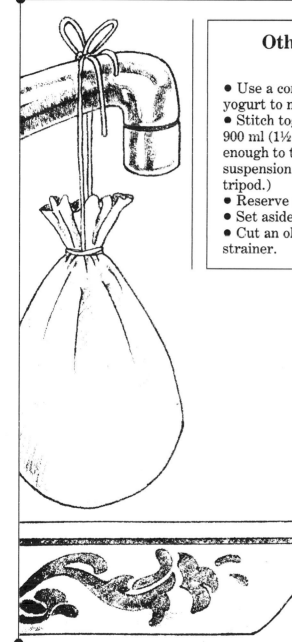

Other Ways For Draining Yogurt to Make Yogurt Cheese

● Use a commercial yogurt maker with an attachment for draining the yogurt to make yogurt cheese.

● Stitch together a muslin bag with a drawstring large enough to hold 900 ml (1½ pints) of homemade yogurt. Make the drawstring long enough to tie on a kitchen tap or to use with some other method of suspension. (A photographer friend suspends his yogurt bags from a tripod.)

● Reserve a new white, thin cotton sock for draining yogurt.

● Set aside a new large linen or cotton handkerchief to line a colander.

● Cut an old but clean cotton T-shirt large enough to line a colander or strainer.

WHITE CHEESE
(Jiban)

Jiban, which means "cheese" in Arabic, is an easy-to-make, fresh white cheese curd, which is either creamy or firm, depending on how much moisture is removed.

This version is a fresh natural product thickened into curds with yogurt and lemon juice. It is then drained, kneaded to a smooth texture, seasoned, shaped, tied into cheesecloth, and marinated in garlicky olive oil. Or, if you like, you can make a feta-like cheese by removing more moisture, forming it into patties, and marinating it in it's own salted whey. (See variation below.)

3.4 litres (6 pints) milk
225 ml (8 fl oz) yogurt, preferably
    homemade, see page 32
20 ml (4 tsp) fresh lemon juice
Salt, to taste
Optional ingredients (see below)
100 ml (4 fl oz) olive oil
2 skinned garlic cloves, cut in half

Optional Ingredients

30 ml (2 tbsp) finely chopped black
    Greek or green olives, squeezed in
    a towel to remove excess moisture.
30 ml (2 tbsp) any favourite finely
    chopped fresh herb such as
    coriander, chives, or dill or 15 ml
    (1 tbsp) finely chopped fresh basil
15 ml (1 tbsp) or more to taste, finely
    chopped green chillies
Freshly ground black pepper or
    cayenne, to taste.

1. Heat the milk in a large saucepan over medium-high heat, stirring occasionally, until it comes to a full boil, about 15 to 20 minutes.

2. Stir in the yogurt and blend thoroughly. Add the lemon juice and boil about 1½ minutes longer, without stirring until the curd separates from the yellowish whey. The milk will foam as it boils.

3. Remove the milk-yogurt mixture from the heat and cool to lukewarm, about 15 minutes.

4. Line a colander with 4 single layers of cheesecloth. Pour the curds and whey into the colander. (Reserve the whey if you wish to make a feta-like cheese.)

5. Let the cheese drain until most of the moisture is removed, about 20 minutes. (It is important to leave some moisture in the curds to aid in the kneading process and to give the cheese a creamy smooth texture.) Bring the corners of the cheesecloth together and squeeze the cheese until it is soft, yet firm.

6. Remove the cheesecloth and place the cheese on a large platter. Salt to taste and knead it with your fingers until the texture is smooth, about 3 to 5 minutes. Add any optional ingredients, if desired.

7. Shape the cheese into 2.5×6.5 cm (1×2½ inch) patties. Tie each patty in a square of double-thickness cheesecloth to hold the curds firmly together. Place them in a shallow dish and add the oil and garlic cloves. Cover and marinate in the refrigerator, turning the cheese occasionally, for at least 2 hours before serving.

8.   Remove from the refrigerator an hour before serving to bring out the full flavour of the cheese.

9.   To store, refrigerate, covered, for up to 1 week, adding more oil, if necessary, to keep the cheese moist.

Makes 8 patties.

Variation *Feta-like Cheese:*
1.   Reverse the whey as it is drained from the curds. See step 4 above. Season it with salt (600 ml (1 pint) of whey to 30 ml (2 tbsp) salt).

2.   Remove most of the moisture from the curds, leaving just enough to mould and shape the cheese into firm, smooth patties. Salt the cheese, if desired, and shape into 2 large or 4 small patties. It is not necessary to wrap the patties in cheesecloth as above.

3.   Cover and store the cheese in the whey-brine solution in the refrigerator for up to 2 weeks.

Lazy Mediterranean Breakfasts

1. Apricot nectar
Minted Yogurt Cheese drizzled
   with olive oil
Herbed Zahter Pitas
Tomato and Onion Salad
Cucumber slices and
   marinated black Greek
   olives
Buttered Basic Pita
Baked Ruby Quince with
   Walnuts
Coffee or Tea

2. Orange Yogurt Shake
Fresh figs
Herb-Scrambled Eggs in
   Yogurt-Cheese-Spread
   Poppy-Seed Pitas
Thinly sliced minted tomatoes
Coffee or Tea

3. Peach Yogurt Shake
Sliced oranges with orange-
   blossom syrup
Capered Smoked Salmon and
   Cheese with buttered Pita
   Toast
Butter and fresh homemade
   preserves
Griddle-Baked Pitas
Coffee or Tea

PICKER UPPERS

 Picker Upper is an appetizer, a snack, an hors d'oeuvre, a tid-bit—whatever you label it, it is fabulous finger food.

Translating the Picker Upper into Middle Eastern hospitality is to explain the *meze*, the Arabic version of Western cocktails with hors d'oeuvres. The *meze*, served at the beginning of a meal, might be a simple bowl of olives and a crock of yogurt cheese served with pita. Or, more likely, it is a lavish spread with a range of dips, tarts, triangles, pies and crudités plus a liberal supply of warm pitas which scoop up everything so well. The *meze* is a celebration in its own right and best describes the very essence of Middle Eastern hospitality, an opportunity to "break bread" with friends, a time for easy conversation and good food. In the centre of it all is pita—baskets full of wedges, crisps, and soft little loaves that work so well with this fare—for pita is not only a bread but an essential eating tool.

The dishes are piquant, tangy, and earthy. Most of them can be prepared in advance and presented with very little last-minute fuss which works perfectly for casual European lifestyles. Try my Middle-Eastern classics such as *Baba Ghanouge*, and Pita Pyramids and dabble with all the other unusual dishes I've included such as Open-Faced Goat Cheese Pita Tarts. Pita is the definitive *picker upper*.

HUMMUS BI TAHINI
(Chickpea Purée)

Hummus Bi Tahini is perhaps the most well known of all the Middle Eastern appetizers. A purée of chickpeas seasoned with Tahini, lemon juice, and garlic, *Hummus* is at once a dip, a spread, a pita filling, or a sandwich topping. Here I've added lots of lemon juice to enliven the subtle flavours. If you like a more spicy *hummus* add cayenne pepper to taste or serve crushed dried chilli flakes as an accompaniment. Or, try using a little cumin for a more exotic variation. While I've given you a choice of using either canned or dried chickpeas, the dried peas have a more natural, nutty taste.

60 ml (4 tbsp) tahini (sesame seed paste; recipe follows)
90 ml (6 tbsp) fresh lemon juice
90–120 ml (6–8 tbsp) warm water
1 clove garlic, chopped
150 g (5 oz) dried chickpeas, cooked and drained (see note) or 396 g (14 oz) can chickpeas, drained and rinsed
2.5 ml (½ tsp) salt
Freshly ground black pepper, to taste
Olive oil (garnish)
Chopped fresh parsley (garnish)
Wholemeal Honey Pitas, page 23, cut into wedges

1.   Put the tahini, lemon juice, water, and garlic into a blender or a food processor fitted with the metal blade. Cover and process until smooth.

2.   With the machine running, gradually add the chickpeas, salt, and pepper, processing until the mixture is the consistency of a very thick paste. If necessary, stop the machine and scrape down the sides with a spatula.

The mixture will thicken when it is refrigerated, so if it seems too thick when you're finished processing it, add up to 120 ml (8 tbsp) more water and process again. Taste to correct seasonings.

3.   Put the *hummus* into a bowl and refrigerate, covered, to chill. Before serving, drizzle with olive oil and garnish with the chopped parsley. Surround with freshly made pita wedges.

To store, refrigerate, covered, for up to 1 week, or freeze for up to 3 months.

Makes about 450 g (1 lb).

Note: To cook dried chickpeas, put 150 g (5 oz) dried chickpeas in a medium bowl, cover with water almost to the top of the bowl, and soak overnight. Drain, put in a saucepan, and cover with fresh water. Cover and bring to a boil, reduce heat, and cook until soft, about 1 hour. Drain and cool. Makes 350 g (12 oz) cooked chickpeas.

HOMEMADE TAHINI
(Sesame Seed Paste)

While Tahini is readily available in health food stores, Middle Eastern groceries, and even most supermarkets today, it is also very easy to make your own.

550 g (1¼ lb) sesame seeds
60–120 ml (4–8 tbsp) vegetable oil

1. Preheat the oven to 180°C (350°F) mark 4.

2. Spread the sesame seeds on a shallow baking tray and bake, shaking frequently, until fragrant, 8 to 10 minutes. Do not brown. Cool.

3. Put the sesame seeds in a blender or food processor fitted with the metal blade. Add the vegetable oil. Process to a smooth paste, about 5 minutes. Add more oil if necessary, to bring the paste to a thick pouring consistency. Tahini will keep stored in a tightly covered jar in the refrigerator for several months.

Makes about 600 ml (1 pint).

HUMMUS GUACAMOLE

For today's eclectic palates, here is a combination of *Hummus Bi Tahini* and Mexican guacamole. Oven-baked pita crisps make marvellous accompaniments instead of the usual tortilla chips. The lemon juice in the *Hummus* complements the subtle flavour of the avocado and helps it to retain its natural colour.

1 ripe avocado, peeled
1 recipe Hummus Bi Tahini, page 40
1 spring onion, finely chopped
1 small ripe tomato, finely chopped
15 ml (1 tbsp) finely chopped hot
    green chillies
Olive oil (garnish)
Chopped fresh coriander (garnish)
Parmesan Pita Crisps, page 28

1. Scoop the avocado into a medium bowl and mash with a fork. Add the *hummus bi tahini* and blend thoroughly.

2. Gently stir in the onion, tomato, and chillies. Taste to correct seasonings. You may want to add more fresh lemon juice, garlic, salt, and pepper, than is called for in the recipe for *hummus bi tahini*.

3. Put the dip into a serving dish and refrigerate, covered, to chill. Before serving, drizzle with olive oil and garnish with chopped coriander. Offer plenty of Parmesan pita crisps for scooping up this dip.

4. To store, follow the directions for *hummus bi tahini*.

Makes about 700 g (1½ lb).

HOT HUMMUS AND FETA CHEESE

Serving *Hummus Bi Tahini* hot with feta cheese and chillies adds a whole new dimension to this versatile dip. While it is sensational with warm pita wedges or pita toast, it is equally good with cool, crunchy crudités.

1 recipe Hummus Bi Tahini, page 40
3 spring onions, chopped
150 g (5 oz) crumbled feta cheese
90 ml (6 tbsp) finely chopped fresh coriander
5–10 ml (1–2 tsp) mild chilli powder
30 ml (2 tbsp) olive oil
Finely chopped spring onions (garnish)
Sesame Pita Crisps, page 28

1. Put the *hummus* in a medium bowl and fold in the onions, feta cheese, coriander, and chilli powder. Blend thoroughly. Taste to correct seasonings.

2. Heat the olive oil in a fondue dish. Add the seasoned *hummus* and stir until the mixture is hot and bubbly, about 5 to 10 minutes.

3. Serve warm in the fondue dish garnished with the chopped onions. Surround with pita crisps.

4. To store, refrigerate, covered, for up to 1 week.

Makes about 700 g (1½ lb).

A Middle-Eastern *Meze* Spread

Baskets of freshly baked Basic, Wholemeal Honey and Griddle-Baked Pitas
Crudités: celery and cucumber sticks, radishes, tomato wedges
Yogurt Cheese Ball rolled in parsley and drizzled with olive oil
Hummus Bi Tahini
Baba Ghanouge
Piquant Pickled Turnips
Bulgur and Lamb Tartare
Marinated Artichokes with Peppers
Fried Aubergine and Courgette with Taratour
Fluted Pita Meat Pies
Tabbouleh
Pistachio Nuts
Fresh fruit in season: figs, persimmons, pomegranates, apricots
Turkish Coffee

HERBED HUMMUS WITH PISTACHIOS

This unorthodox yet interesting variation on a *hummus* theme adds a welcome contrast of flavour and texture. The pungent taste of freshly chopped watercress and coriander and the crunchiness of the pistachios meld together to bring out the nuttiness of the puréed chickpeas. After sampling this recipe, perhaps you will be inspired to try your own favourite combinations of fresh herbs and nuts with *hummus*.

1 recipe Hummus Bi Tahini, page 40
90 ml (6 tbsp) finely chopped watercress
90 ml (6 tbsp) finely chopped fresh coriander
40 g (1½ oz) chopped pistachio nuts
Olive oil (garnish)
Pistachio nuts (garnish)
Poppy-Seed Pitas, page 22, cut into wedges

1. Put the *hummus* in a medium bowl and fold in the watercress and coriander. Blend thoroughly. Taste to correct seasonings. Refrigerate, covered, to chill.

2. Add the chopped pistachio nuts and mix thoroughly. Turn into a serving dish and drizzle with olive oil. Garnish with the additional nuts. Serve with poppy-seed pita wedges.

3. To store, follow the directions for *hummus bi tahini*, page 40.

Makes about 700 g (1½ lb).

BABA GHANOUGE
(Aubergine Sesame Purée)

This sharp smoky purée of aubergine and Tahini blended with just the right amount of lemon juice and freshly crushed garlic is redolent of the flavours of the Middle East. Translated literally, *Baba Ghanouge* means "pampered father" or "spoiled father," a phrase, no doubt, coined long ago by loving wives anxious to coddle their beloved husbands or fathers. Now, pamper yourself and your guests with this version. Chances are, you'll come up with some of your own variations, too. Serve it as a dip for scooping with pita wedges or as a filling for a pita sandwich!

1 large (about 700 g/1 lb) aubergine
60 ml (4 tbsp) tahini (sesame seed paste), page 41
60 ml (4 tbsp) warm water
45 ml (3 tbsp) fresh lemon juice, or more, to taste
1 clove garlic, crushed
Salt and freshly ground black pepper, to taste
Olive oil (garnish)
Parsley sprigs (garnish)
Wheat-Germ Honey Pitas, page 24, cut into wedges

1. Preheat the grill.

2. Pierce one side of the aubergine with a fork. Place, pierced side up, on a foil-covered grill pan set on a rack so that the top of the aubergine is about 12.5–15 cm (5–6 inches) from the heat source. Grill until the top is charred and starts to blister and the bottom is soft to the touch, about 30 to 45 minutes.

3. Remove and let cool until the aubergine can be handled easily, about 10 minutes. Slit the softened side and scoop the pulp into a medium bowl, scraping all the flesh from the inner skin. Pour off any darkened liquid and remove any large cluster of seeds as both may impart an unpleasant bitter taste. Mash the pulp well with a fork.

4. Mix the tahini with the warm water until smooth and whitened. Add the mixture to the aubergine along with the lemon juice, garlic, salt, and pepper. Mix until pale in colour and smooth. Taste to correct seasonings.

5. Transfer to a serving bowl, and refrigerate, covered, to chill. Before serving, drizzle with olive oil and garnish with parsley. Serve with wheat-germ honey pita wedges.

6. To store, follow the directions for *hummus bi tahini*, page 40.

Makes about 450 g (1 lb).

Variation *Aubergine Caviar:* Omit the tahini and water. Add 3 finely chopped spring onions and 30 ml (2 tbsp) olive oil to the remaining ingredients and follow the directions above. You may add other chopped vegetables such as tomatoes or green pepper. Taste to correct seasonings. Refrigerate, covered, to chill.

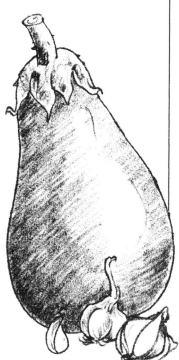

Selecting and Preparing Aubergine

Select aubergines that are firm, heavy for their size, cylindrical in shape, smooth, and glossy. While the royal dark-purple variety is the most commonly available, aubergines also come in white, reddish, and yellowish tints, and even in a mottled stripe.

Aubergines are characteristically porous and contain a lot of water which can make them bitter. Depending upon the recipe to be prepared, there are several things you can do to avoid this bitterness.

• If you're grilling aubergine, pour off the darkened liquid that collects.

• If you're frying or baking, first slice the aubergine and layer the slices on kitchen paper, lightly salting each side as you layer the aubergine. Cover the top with another layer of kitchen paper, pat down lightly and let the aubergine stand for about an hour to remove the excess moisture. Then pat the aubergine slices completely dry with fresh kitchen paper.

OLIVE-LACED BABA GHANOUGE

In this recipe, the aubergine-tahini blend is especially distinctive with the addition of olives and *zahter,* an herb blend of marjoram, thyme, toasted sesame seeds, and sumac.

1 recipe Baba Ghanouge, page 44
175 g (6 oz) pitted and finely
　chopped black Greek olives
2.5–5 ml (½–1 tsp) zahter (see
　page 166 for a substitute)
Olive oil (garnish)
Chopped fresh parsley (garnish)
Basic Pitas, page 21, cut into
　wedges

1. Put the *baba ghanouge* in a medium bowl and fold in the chopped olives and *zahter.* Blend thoroughly. Taste to correct seasonings.

2. Transfer to a serving dish and refrigerate, covered, to chill. Before serving, drizzle with olive oil and garnish with chopped parsley. Serve with the pita wedges.

To store, follow the directions for *hummus bi tahini,* page 40.

Makes about 700 g (1½ lb).

CHICKEN LIVER PATE

Crispy toasted pita wedges are perfect for scooping up this unusual Chicken Liver Pâté. The classic French appetizer boasts a Mediterranean twist with a hefty measure of anchovy paste and Yogurt Cheese.

150 g (5 oz) softened butter
900 g (2 lb) chicken livers
1 medium chopped onion
100 ml (4 fl oz) Cognac
175 ml (6 fl oz) firm Yogurt Cheese,
*　　page 33*
45 ml (3 tbsp) anchovy paste
2.5 ml (½ tsp) salt
2.5 ml (½ tsp) crumbled dried thyme
90 ml (6 tbsp) finely chopped fresh
*　　parsley*
2 hard-boiled eggs, yolks and whites
*　　sieved separately (garnish)*
Plain Pita Toast, page 28

1.　Melt 25 g (1 oz) of the butter in a frying pan. Add the chicken livers and onion and sauté over medium heat, stirring frequently, until the livers are brown on the outside but still pink inside, 5 minutes.

2.　With a slotted spoon, remove the livers and onions to a blender or food processor fitted with the metal blade. Reduce the remaining juices in the pan by half and add to the chicken livers.

3.　Heat the Cognac in a small saucepan over medium heat until reduced to 60 ml (4 tbsp); be careful not to let it ignite. Add it to the livers. Add the remaining butter, yogurt cheese, anchovy paste, salt and thyme. Process the mixture until completely blended and smooth. Transfer to a bowl and refrigerate, covered, until firm.

4.　Divide the pâté in half. Shape each half into a cylinder and roll both in the chopped parsley to coat. Place the pâté rolls on a platter and garnish with the sieved egg yolks and whites. Serve with pita toast.

Makes two 15×6.5 cm (6×2½ inch) logs.

An Elegant Cocktail Party

Buttered Pita Toast
Capered Smoked Salmon and
　Cheese
Caviar surrounded by lemon
　wedges, chopped hard-
　boiled egg, and chopped
　red onion
Chicken Liver Pâté
Chilled Champagne

ORIENTAL PRAWN AND BLACK BEAN DIP

Everytime I go to our favourite Chinese restaurant in New York's Chinatown, I ask the chef to create a special version of Prawn and Black Bean Sauce. I always insist that he sliver the ginger and sprinkle it generously with finely chopped spring onions which perfectly complement the flavours of the prawn and black bean sauce. One day I decided to use these ingredients as a dip in combination with creamy Yogurt Cheese. Here I use plain black beans rather than the fermented Chinese variety, which would overpower the delightful tanginess of the Yogurt Cheese.

1 recipe Yogurt Cheese, page 33
450 g (1 lb) cooked prawns
25 g (1 oz) dried black beans, cooked, (see note) or 50 g (2 oz) canned black beans, heated
3 spring onions, finely chopped
5 ml (1 tsp) finely slivered fresh ginger
1 clove garlic, crushed
2.5–5 ml (½–1 tsp) soy sauce
Salt and freshly ground black pepper, to taste
Chopped spring onions (garnish)
Wholemeal Honey Pitas, page 23, cut into wedges

1. Combine all the ingredients except the onions for garnish and pita wedges in a medium bowl. Mix thoroughly and taste to correct seasonings. Refrigerate, covered, to chill.

2. Transfer the dip to a serving bowl and garnish with the chopped onions. Serve with warm wholemeal pita wedges.

Makes about 800 g (1¾ lb).

Note: Cook black beans by first rinsing them in cold running water and discarding any stones or shrivelled beans. Cover each 175 g (6 oz) of dry beans with 600 ml (1 pint) of water and let stand for 12 hours or overnight. Cook the beans in the water they have soaked in until they are tender, about 1 to 1½ hours. The beans should be soft, yet firm, not mushy. Soak the 25 g (1 oz) of dry beans called for in this recipe in about 300 ml (½ pint) of water for at least 12 hours. Cook as above; they should be ready in 35 to 45 minutes.

How to Cook Prawns

Bring a large saucepan of water to a boil. Add a few parsley sprigs, peppercorns, 2 small bay leaves, and a dash of salt. Add the prawns and bring the water back to boiling. Immediately reduce the heat to low and simmer until the prawns are a delicate pink, 2 to 3 minutes. To ensure that the prawns will be tender, never overcook them and never cook them over high heat. Drain and refrigerate to chill. (Do not plunge the prawns into ice water to chill as this will make them tough and waterlogged.) Shell and devein.

TARAMASALATA
(Greek Fish Roe Salad)

Tart and tangy, this dip is a superb addition to a Middle Eastern *meze* spread. Don't forget to serve some juicy black Greek olives accompanied by cucumber and celery strips for dipping. Buttered pita toast ties everything together.

3 slices white bread, crusts removed
45 ml (3 tbsp) water
90 ml (6 tbsp) smoked cods roe
30 ml (2 tbsp) chopped onion
175 ml (6 fl oz) olive oil
45 ml (3 tbsp) fresh lemon juice
1 small clove garlic (optional)
Chopped fresh parsley (garnish)
Buttered Pita Toast, page 28
Black Greek olives
Celery and cucumber strips

1.　Sprinkle the bread with the water to soften, then squeeze dry.

2.　Place the bread, roe, onion, 50 ml (2 fl oz) oil, lemon juice, and garlic in a blender and blend until smooth.

3.　With the machine running, add the remaining oil in a slow steady stream. Continue blending until the mixture is creamy.

4.　Put the dip into a bowl and refrigerate, covered, to chill. Before serving, garnish with the chopped parsley. Surround with the buttered pita toast, black Greek olives, and celery and cucumber strips.

Makes about 350 g (12 oz).

CAPERED SMOKED SALMON

This pastel-coloured spread of salmon and capers is given a Middle Eastern accent with the use of Yogurt Cheese as a base. It is a special treat with crisp Buttered Pita Toast and a glass or two of Champagne.

1 recipe Yogurt Cheese, page 33
　(omit the salt)
75 g (3 oz) smoked salmon, cut into
　julienne strips
2 spring onions, finely chopped
5 ml (1 tsp) fresh lemon juice
15–30 ml (1–2 tbsp) capers, finely
　chopped, to taste
Freshly ground black pepper, to
　taste
Lemon wedges (garnish)
Buttered Pita Toast, page 28

1.　Combine all the ingredients except the lemon wedges and pita toast in a medium bowl. Mix gently until smooth; taste to correct seasonings. Refrigerate, covered, to chill.

2.　Transfer to a serving bowl. Garnish with the lemon wedges and surround with buttered pita toast.

Makes about 700 g (1½ lb).

PITA TEA SANDWICHES

For an unusual tea party, offer pots of freshly brewed Mint Tea, page 158, and Spiced Aniseed Tea, page 27, and a tray of dainty pita tea sandwiches. Pitas filled with a choice of savoury and sweet fillings are perfect for the occasion. Cut large pitas into triangles. Spread them first with Yogurt Cheese, and add an array of enticing fillings. (For the sweet or fruity varieties, use unsalted Yogurt Cheese.)

- Sliced avocado and chopped spring onions
- Cucumber and smoked salmon
- Watercress sprigs and sliced hard-boiled egg
- Coriander sprigs and tiny boiled prawns
- Capers and smoked chicken
- Rocket and smoked ham
- Chopped black Greek olives
- Tomatoes sprinkled with chopped fresh basil
- Sliced radishes and prawn or lobster salad
- Flaked crabmeat and sliced papaya
- Homemade raspberry or blackberry preserves
- Sliced strawberries or peaches
- Chopped raisins or dates and walnuts or pecans
- Chopped dried or sliced fresh figs and thinly sliced orange.

If you make the sandwiches ahead, top them with a very lightly dampened double-thickness of kitchen paper and wrap in kitchen foil or cling film. Store in the refrigerator to chill. To serve, arrange them on a tray and offer at room temperature for peak flavour.

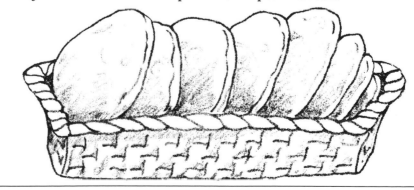

PRAWN WITH AVOCADO-SESAME SAUCE

This prawn dressed in a lemony avocado-sesame sauce is quite different—tart and nutty with a decided taste of the sea. Serve it as an appetizer accompanied by soft fresh pita wedges or use it as a filling for a lettuce-lined pita pocket topped with thinly sliced tomato. Save a little dressing to drizzle on top!

1 medium ripe avocado, peeled and mashed
45 ml (3 tbsp) tahini (sesame seed paste), page 41
1 clove garlic, crushed
60 ml (4 tbsp) fresh lemon juice or more, to taste
Salt and freshly ground black pepper, to taste
30–60 ml (2–4 tbsp) water
90 ml (6 tbsp) finely chopped fresh parsley
700 g (1½ lb) cooked prawns
Wholemeal Sesame Pitas, page 24, cut into wedges

1. Mix the avocado, tahini, garlic, lemon juice, salt, and pepper in a large bowl; add water gradually (up to 60 ml/4 tbsp) until the mixture is of a thick pouring consistency. Taste to correct seasonings.

2. Blend in the chopped parsley. Add the prawns and toss gently to coat. Refrigerate, covered, to chill.

3. Place on a serving platter and surround with wholemeal sesame pita wedges.

Makes 6 to 8 servings.

Patio Barbecue

Olive-Laced Baba Ghanouge with Basic Pita wedges
Prawn with Avocado-Sesame Sauce and Wholemeal Sesame Pita wedges
Yogurt-Marinated Shish Kebabs in Basic Pitas
Herb-Grilled Chicken and Onion on Herbed Zahter Pitas
Minted Potato Salad
Classic Mediterranean Salad
Pita and Halvah
Iced beer
Coffee

KIBBEH
(Middle-Eastern Meatballs)

The recipe that follows is a basic mixture for cooked *Kibbeh*. This varies slightly from Bulgur and Lamb Tartare (*Kibbeh Nayee*) in that I've included 50 g (2 oz) less bulgur per 450 g (1 lb) of minced meat so that the cooked dish has a firmer texture for eating by hand. The first time you serve these little nuggets of goodness you'll find they'll be devoured and your guests will come back for more!

150 g (5 oz) bulgur
450 g (1 lb) minced lean lamb (all fat removed)
1 small onion, grated
1.25 ml (¼ tsp) ground allspice
1.25 ml (¼ tsp) ground cinnamon
Salt and freshly ground black pepper, to taste
Vegetable oil, for frying
Basic Pitas, page 21, cut into wedges
Yogurt-Garlic Sauce (recipe below)

1. Rinse the bulgur and place it in a medium bowl. Cover with cool water and let soak until it is tender to the bite, 20 to 30 minutes. Drain thoroughly and squeeze out any excess water. Fluff to separate the grains.

2. Combine the lamb, onion, allspice, cinnamon, salt and pepper in a large bowl. Mix thoroughly.

3. Prepare a bowl of ice and water. Keeping your hands cold and moist by dipping them into the bowl of ice and water, gradually add the bulgur to the

About Kibbeh

Kibbeh is the national dish of both Lebanon and Syria. This distinctive and healthful combination of finely minced lean lamb, bulgur, onions, and spices is the basis of many wonderful dishes that star with pita. These dishes are made into various shapes and sizes, are filled or layered, then fried, baked, or even eaten raw, much like steak tartare. Ask your butcher to mince lean meat very finely or, if you wish, you may do it in your food processor. I have included all the popular *kibbeh* recipes that complement pita and that are always found on a *meze* spread. With the exception of Bulgur and Lamb Tartare (*Kibbeh Nayee*), all these *kibbeh* dishes may be made ahead and refrigerated, covered, for up to 3 days or frozen for up to 3 months. To serve, thaw in the refrigerator overnight. Reheat in a preheated 170° (325°F) mark 3 oven until warmed through, about 10 to 15 minutes.

lamb, mixture, kneading thoroughly after each addition. Knead the mixture for another minute after all the bulgur has been added. Taste to correct seasonings.

4.   Divide the *kibbeh* into 36 portions and shape into smooth balls. Refrigerate the balls, covered, in a large bowl until firm, 30 minutes to 1 hour.

5.   Pour the oil to a depth of 1 cm (½ inch) in a large frying pan and heat until hot but not smoking.

Working in batches add the meatballs in a single layer and cook over medium-high heat, turning often until evenly browned and cooked through, 5 to 8 minutes. Drain on kitchen paper. Add more oil to the pan, if necessary, to cook the remaining meatballs.

6.   Serve warm with pita wedges and a bowl of yogurt-garlic sauce for dipping.

Makes 36 meatballs.

YOGURT-GARLIC SAUCE

Yogurt-Garlic Sauce is an especially versatile sauce which goes equally well with meat, fish, and vegetables. Use it both as a dip or as a dressing for pita sandwiches.

225 ml (8 fl oz) natural yogurt, preferably homemade, page 32
1 clove garlic, crushed
5 ml (1 tsp) fresh lemon juice
15 ml (1 tbsp) finely chopped fresh parsley
Salt and freshly ground black pepper, to taste

Combine all the ingredients in a small bowl and stir gently to blend. Refrigerate, covered, to chill.

Makes 225 ml (8 fl oz).

Variations

Yogurt-Mint Sauce: Substitute 15 ml (1 tbsp) chopped fresh mint or 5 ml (1 tsp) crumbled dried mint for the parsley.

Yogurt-Cucumber Sauce: Add 75 g (3 oz) finely chopped cucumber to the main recipe.

BULGUR AND LAMB TARTARE

(Kibbeh Nayee)

Translated literally, *Kibbeh Nayee* means naked or raw *kibbeh*. Rather like a rough-textured steak tartare, *Kibbeh Nayee* is always found on the *meze* or appetizer tray in a Middle Eastern home or restaurant. In order to savour the fresh taste of lamb and bulgur, I rarely season this version with anything more than salt and pepper, although I've suggested an optional measure of cinnamon or allspice. Offer freshly ground black pepper as an accompaniment as well as a cruet of fruity olive oil. Soft pita wedges are a must.

175 g (6 oz) bulgur
450 g (1 lb) minced lean lamb (all fat removed)
50 g (2 oz) grated red onion
Salt and pepper, to taste
Ground allspice or cinnamon to taste (optional)
15–30 ml (1–2 tbsp) iced water
Olive oil (garnish)

Chopped fresh parsley or mint (garnish)
Basic Pitas, page 21, cut into wedges

1. Rinse the bulgur and place it in a medium bowl. Cover with cool water and let soak until it is tender to the bite, 20 to 30 minutes. Drain thoroughly and squeeze out any

Presentation for Bulgur and Lamb Tartare

It is true that we begin every dining experience with our eyes and with Bulgur and Lamb Tartare (*Kibbeh Nayee*) there is no exception. Try experimenting with these and other presentations. Always offer pita wedges as an accompaniment, of course, along with a cruet of olive oil and a pepper mill.

• Grease a small loaf tin with olive oil and firmly press the chilled *Kibbeh Nayee* into the pan. Turn it over to unmould and place it on a serving platter or board. Garnish with chopped crisp spring onions and toasted pine nuts. Offer a knife and suggest guests slice into 1 cm (½ inch) servings.

• Shape into orange-sized balls and roll them in finely chopped parsley or a light sprinkling of freshly ground black peppercorns. Serve them on a lettuce-lined dish with a spoon.

• Shape into individual walnut-sized balls and mound them on a serving platter. Garnish with finely chopped parsley and spring onions. Drizzle with olive oil.

excess water. Fluff to separate the grains.

2. Combine the lamb, onion, salt, pepper, and allspice or cinnamon in a large bowl. Mix thoroughly.

3. Prepare a bowl of ice and water. Keeping your hands cold and moist by dipping them into the bowl of ice and water, gradually add the bulgur to the lamb mixture, kneading thoroughly after each addition. Add 15–30 ml (1–2 tbsp) of the iced water to the mixture and continue kneading until it is slightly softened. Taste to correct seasonings.

4. Shape the *kibbeh nayee* into a mound on a serving platter. Refrig-erate, covered, for at least 1 hour. Depress a pattern on the surface with the tines of a fork; drizzle with olive oil and garnish with fresh parsley or mint. Serve with fresh pita wedges.

Makes about 8 servings.

Variation
Pine Nut and Onion Tartare: Arrange the *kibbeh nayee* into 12 small round or oval patties. Press the edges with the tines of a fork. Top each with minced onion and toasted whole pine nuts. Drizzle with olive oil and garnish with chopped parsley.

BAKED MEAT DIAMONDS
(Kibbeh Sinayee)

Kibbeh Sinayee means *Kibbeh* in a pan. Most Middle Easterners serve this traditional dish as an entrée. Here we suggest serving these diamond-shaped portions as an appetizer with pita wedges. They're sure to bring raves.

1 recipe Kibbeh (Middle Eastern
   Meatballs), page 51, prepared up
   to step 3
25 g (1 oz) butter
1 medium onion, chopped
450 g (1 lb) minced lamb
30 ml (2 tbsp) pine nuts
2.5 ml (½ tsp) ground cinnamon
Salt and pepper, to taste
30 ml (2 tbsp) Yogurt Cheese,
   page 33
90 ml (6 tbsp) clarified butter,
   melted (see note)

Wholemeal Honey Pitas, page 23,
   cut into wedges

1. Refrigerate the *kibbeh*, covered, until ready to bake.

2. To prepare the filling, melt the butter in a frying pan. Add the onions and sauté over medium heat, until tender and transparent, about 5 minutes. Add the lamb, pine nuts, cinnamon, salt, and pepper. Cook, stirring constantly, until the meat is

crumbled and lightly browned, about 15 minutes.

3. Remove from the heat and stir in the yogurt cheese. Blend until well mixed. Cool in the pan at room temperature.

4. Preheat the oven to 200°C (400°F) mark 6.

5. Thoroughly grease the bottom and sides of a 20.5 or 23 cm (8 or 9 inch) square or round baking dish with 30 ml (2 tbsp) of the melted clarified butter. Prepare a bowl of ice and water. Place half the *kibbeh* in the pan, spreading it evenly. Pat the surface smooth. Dip your hands in the ice and water to prevent the *kibbeh* from sticking to your fingers.

Cover with the filling, spreading it evenly. Spread the remaining *kibbeh* to cover the filling and pat the surface smooth.

6. With your forefinger, press a hole in the centre and each corner of the dish to help disperse the butter during baking. With a sharp knife, score into diamond shapes. Score completely through the mixture diagonally at 4 cm (1½ inch) intervals across the dish. Diagonally crisscross scores over these to make the diamond shapes. See illustration. Drizzle the *kibbeh* with the remaining clarified butter.

7. Bake until browned and firm, 30 to 45 minutes. Remove and let cool to lukewarm.

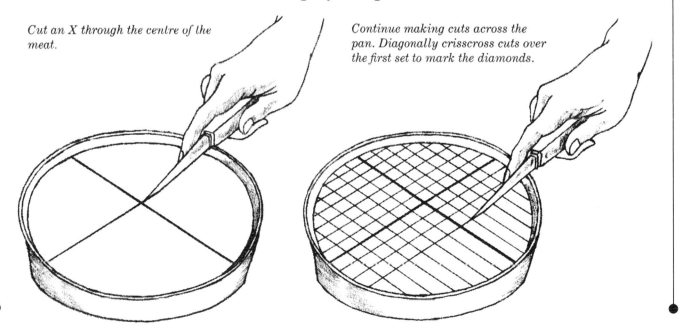

Cut an X through the centre of the meat.

Continue making cuts across the pan. Diagonally crisscross cuts over the first set to mark the diamonds.

8. Cut out the diamond shapes. Remove from the pan with a long thin spatula. Serve warm with wholemeal honey pita wedges.

Makes about 40 diamonds.

Note: To clarify butter, melt unsalted or salted butter in a heavy saucepan over very low heat. Simmer slowly to allow the dairy solids and salt, if any, to rise to the top. Skim constantly until all the dairy solids have been removed and the butter is clear. (Save the skimmings to season freshly cooked vegetables). I usually clarify about 1.8–2.3 kg (4–5 lb) of butter at a time. It will keep refrigerated indefinitely, although it need not be refrigerated for short-term use. Once heated, butter develops its own built-in preservative.

Variation

Stuffed Kibbeh (Kibbeh Ahkras): Instead of baking the *kibbeh* with the filling and cutting into diamond shapes, make stuffed meat balls. *Ahkras* means oval in Arabic and the children in Middle Eastern homes often refer to these stuffed delicacies as footballs since the most skilful cooks taper the ends to resemble an American football!

1. Divide the *kibbeh* into 18 to 20 balls.

2. Prepare the filling for Baked Meat Diamonds, up to step 3.

3. Dipping your hands in a bowl of ice and water to prevent sticking, press a cavity about 4–5 cm (1½–2 inches) deep into each ball. Divide the filling evenly among the balls and place 1 portion into each cavity.

4. Pinch the openings closed and shape into balls, cakes or ovals, about 5–6.5 cm (2–2½ inches) in diameter.

5. Pour the oil to a depth of 1 cm (½ inch) in a frying pan and heat until hot but not smoking. Working in batches, add the balls in a single layer and cook over medium-high heat, turning often until evenly browned and cooked through, 5 to 8 minutes. Add more oil to the pan if necessary, to cook the remaining balls. Drain on kitchen paper.

6. Serve them as appetizers accompanied by pita wedges and yogurt-garlic sauce, page 52.

Makes 18 to 20 stuffed balls.

While *frying* is a popular method of cookery in the Middle East for meatballs or patties and vegetable slices, *grilling* is an acceptable and preferable substitute for dieters. Brush the patties or vegetables with a little oil before *grilling*.

MEDITERRANEAN PRAWN PATE

(Kibbeh Samak)

This traditional hot-weather dish from the Eastern shores of the Mediterranean is a fragrant blend of prawns, bulgar, coriander and sweet onion pressed on top of a layer of thinly sliced onion and pine nuts, cut into diamond shapes, then baked to a turn. Similar in character to a pâté, it is served at room temperature as an appetizer, a main dish, or as a pita sandwich, topped with Carrot, Orange and Radish Salad, page 94. Make this dish a day in advance as it improves in flavour when refrigerated overnight.

1.5 kg (3¼ lb) medium prawns, shelled and deveined (1.1 kg/2½ lb shelled prawns)
20 ml (4 tsp) salt
Pinch of cinnamon
350 g (12 oz) bulgur
3 large onions
30 ml (2 tbsp) ground coriander
15 ml (1 tbsp) grated orange rind
2.5 ml (½ tsp) pepper
300 ml (½ pint) vegetable oil
50 g (2 oz) pine nuts
Shredded Cos lettuce leaves
Lemon wedges (garnish)
Basic Pitas, page 21, cut into wedges

1. To prepare the prawns, place them in a large bowl and sprinkle lightly with 5 ml (½ tsp) salt and the cinnamon. Toss to coat evenly. Refrigerate, covered, to chill for several hours or overnight. Drain.

2. To prepare the bulgur, rinse the grains and place them in a medium bowl. Cover with cool water and let soak until tender to the bite, 20 to 30 minutes. Drain thoroughly and squeeze out any excess water. Fluff to separate the grains. Refrigerate, covered, until ready to use.

3. To prepare the sliced onions, peel two of the onions, cut them in half lengthwise, then slice them very thin. Place them in a large bowl. Sprinkle lightly with 5 ml (½ tsp) salt and toss to coat evenly. Let stand until they are limp and moist. Squeeze out all the water and set aside.

4. Skin the remaining onion and cut it into quarters.

5. Place half of the prawns and two onion quarters in a food processor fitted with the metal blade. Process carefully to a medium texture (or mince in a mincer using the fine cutting wheel). Transfer to a mixing bowl. Repeat with the remaining half of the prawns and onion quarters.

6. Prepare a bowl of ice and water. Add the bulgur to the prawn-onion mixture and knead thoroughly until well blended, keeping your hands cool by dipping them in the bowl of ice and water. Add the coriander, orange rind, the remaining salt, and the pepper. Mix well.

7. Working in two batches, place half the prawn-bulgur mixture in the

food processor and process carefully to a fine texture (or mince the mixture in a mincer as above). Be careful not to overprocess or the pâté mixture will be pasty. Repeat with the remaining mixture. Combine the 2 batches.

8. Preheat the oven to 230°C (450°F) mark 8.

9. To bake and serve the pâté pour 50 ml (2 fl oz) of the oil into a 25.5×38 cm (10×5 inch) baking dish (see note). Coat the bottom and sides thoroughly. Layer the sliced onions and the pine nuts evenly over the bottom of the dish.

10. Scoop up a handful of the prawn-bulgur mixture and flatten it between the palms of both hands. Beginning at one corner of the pan, place the mixture carefully over the onions and pine nuts. Continue with the remaining prawn-bulgur mixture, until the entire layer of onions and nuts is covered to a depth of 1–2 cm (½–¾ inch). Dipping your hands in ice water, pat the surface and edges smooth.

11. With your forefinger, press a hole in the centre and at each corner of the dish to help disperse the oil during baking. With a sharp knife, score the pâté into diamond shapes. Score completely through the pâté diagonally at 4 cm (1½ inch) intervals across the dish. Diagonally criss-cross scores over these to make the diamond shapes. See illustration on page 55. Carefully coat the surface with the remaining oil.

12. Bake until the loaf is golden brown and firm and the oil is bubbling, about 50 to 60 minutes. Remove from the oven and drain the remaining oil from the dish. To retain the moisture, cover the dish with a baking sheet. Let the covered pâté cool completely in the dish.

13. Place the lettuce on a serving platter. Cut out the diamond shapes and remove the pâté from the dish with a long thin spatula; be careful to get all the onions and pine nuts with each piece. Arrange the pâté nut-side-up on the lettuce. Garnish with the lemon wedges. Pass basic pita wedges as an accompaniment.

Makes 10 to 12 servings.

Note: Since the kibbeh should be between 1–2 cm (½–¾ inch) thick when baked, using the right size dish is important. If you vary the dish size, make sure your pâté doesn't get too thick or thin.

SPINACH AND RAISIN TRIANGLES

(Fatayer Sabanich)

For a delicious change of pace, try these tart spinach triangles made with Basic Pita dough. It is important to sprinkle the fresh spinach with salt as the recipe directs. This allows it to wilt so you can squeeze out the water before you prepare the filling. Otherwise, the water will seep out during the baking, making the triangles soggy. This recipe takes a little time, but the results make the effort well worth it. Served warm or cold, Spinach and Raisin Triangles make excellent appetizers and, because they carry well without refrigeration, also make great picnic fare.

900 g (2 lb) fresh spinach, stems trimmed, rinsed, coarsely chopped, and patted dry, or three 300 g (10.6 oz) packets frozen chopped spinach, thawed, squeezed dry, and fluffed to separate
Salt
40–50 g (1½–2 oz) raisins
300 ml (½ pint) fresh lemon juice
1 large onion, finely chopped
100 ml (4 fl oz) olive oil
100 g (4 oz) coarsely chopped walnuts
Freshly ground black pepper, to taste
1 recipe Basic Pita dough, page 21, prepared through step 2
100 ml (4 fl oz) clarified butter, melted, page 56

1.   Place the spinach in a colander. (If you are using fresh spinach, sprinkle lightly with salt and let stand until wilted. Squeeze to remove as much liquid as possible.)

2.   Soak the raisins in boiling water until they are plumped, about 5 to 10 minutes. Drain thoroughly and dry with kitchen paper.

3.   Combine the spinach and raisins with the lemon juice, onion, olive oil, walnuts, and pepper. Taste to correct seasonings. Set aside.

4.   Divide the pita dough into 48 portions and shape each portion into a smooth ball. Place the balls on a floured work surface, and cover with slightly damp tea-towels to keep the surface of the dough damp and moist. Let rest 30 to 45 minutes in a warm draught-free place.

5.   Place 1 rack near the bottom third of the oven and another one just above it. Preheat the oven to 220°C (425°F) mark 7. Lightly grease 2 baking sheets.

6.   Working in 2 batches of 24 pies at a time, gently press each ball flat with your fingers, keeping it well rounded. Flour a work surface and rolling pin. Roll each round of dough into an 8.5 cm (3½ inch) circle.

7.   Divide the spinach mixture equally into 48 portions, about 1½ to 2 rounded tablespoons each, and place 1 portion in the centre of each circle, being careful to drain off most of the

liquid. Pick up the edges and pinch 3 sides of each circle firmly together to form a triangle, sealing the top of the triangle completely. Make certain that all the sides are well sealed to keep the juices from oozing out during baking. See illustration, page 67.

8.   Arrange 12 triangles on each of the 2 greased baking sheets. Lightly brush with clarified butter.

9.   Bake 2 sheets at a time, placing 1 sheet on each pre-positioned oven rack staggering 1 on the right and 1 on the left. Reverse the sheets from the top to bottom oven racks halfway through baking for even heat distribution. Bake until lightly browned, 15 to 20 minutes.

10.   Repeat the process with the remaining 24 rounds of dough and the spinach mixture while the first batch bakes.

11.   Remove the baked triangles from the oven and brush again with the clarified butter. Serve immediately or cool on wire racks and refrigerate, covered, for up to 1 week or freeze for up to 3 months. To serve, thaw in the refrigerator overnight. Serve at room temperature or reheat in a preheated 170°C (325°F) mark 3 oven for 10 to 15 minutes.

12.   Bake the remaining 24 triangles following the same method.

Makes 48 triangles.

Anything-Goes Holiday Buffet

Taramasalata with Buttered
   Pita Toast
Spinach and Feta Triangles
Homemade Roasted Peppers
Mediterranean Prawn Pâté
   with Basic Pita wedges
Chef's Couscous Salad with
   Wheat-Germ Honey Pitas
Curried Spinach, Walnut and
   Orange Salad
Pita Cheese Crêpes with Rose
   Water Syrup
Orangeade with orange-
   blossom water
Coffee or Tea

SPINACH AND FETA TRIANGLES

This traditional filling for a Greek *Spanakopita* stars here as a filling for a pita dough triangle, instead of the very rich butter-laced phyllo dough. Made without butter and eggs, this version is a healthy alternative to a popular appetizer—and tasty too!

900 g (2 lb) fresh spinach, stems trimmed, rinsed, coarsely chopped, and patted dry, or three 300 g (10.6 oz) packets frozen chopped spinach, thawed, squeezed dry, and fluffed to separate
Salt
100 ml (4 fl oz) olive oil
2 medium onions, finely chopped
Freshly ground black pepper, to taste
1.25 ml (¼ tsp) nutmeg, or to taste
45 ml (3 tbsp) snipped fresh dill or 15 ml (1 tbsp) dried dill
275 g (10 oz) ricotta cheese
175 g (6 oz) finely crumbled feta cheese
1 recipe Basic Pita dough, page 21, prepared up to step 2

1. Place the spinach in a colander. (If you are using fresh spinach, sprinkle lightly with salt and let stand until wilted. Squeeze to remove as much liquid as possible.)

2. Heat 50 ml (2 fl oz) of the olive oil in a frying pan. Add the onions and sauté over medium heat until translucent, about 5 minutes. Add the spinach and cook over low heat, stirring constantly, until the mixture is cooked through, about 10 minutes.

Add the pepper and nutmeg. Cool to room temperature.

3. Blend in the dill and ricotta and feta cheeses. Taste to correct seasonings. Refrigerate, covered, until ready to fill the triangles.

4. Divide the pita dough into 48 portions and shape each portion into a smooth ball. Place the balls on a floured work surface and cover with slightly damp tea-towels to keep the surface of the dough damp and moist. Let rest 30 to 45 minutes in a warm draught-free place.

5. Place 1 rack near the bottom third of the oven and another one just above it. Preheat the oven to 220°C (425°F) mark 7. Lightly grease 2 baking sheets.

6. Working in 2 batches of 24 pies at a time, gently press each ball flat with your fingers, keeping it well rounded. Flour a work surface and rolling pin. Roll each round of dough into an 8.5 cm (3½ inch) circle.

7. Divide the spinach mixture equally into 48 portions, about 1 to 2 rounded tablespoons each, and place 1 portion in the centre of each circle. Pick up the edges and pinch 3 sides of

each circle firmly together to form a triangle, sealing the top of the triangle completely. Make certain that all the sides are well sealed to keep the juices from oozing out during baking. See illustration, page 67.

8.   Arrange the 12 triangles on each of the 2 greased baking sheets. Lightly brush with olive oil.

9.   Bake 2 sheets at a time, placing 1 sheet on each pre-positioned oven rack staggering 1 on the right and 1 on the left. Reverse the sheets from the top to bottom oven racks halfway through baking for even heat distribution. Bake until lightly browned, 15 to 20 minutes.

10.   Repeat the process with the remaining 24 rounds of dough and the spinach-cheese mixture while the first batch bakes.

11.   Remove the baked triangles from the oven and brush again with oil. Serve immediately or cool on wire racks and refrigerate, covered, for up to 3 days or freeze for up to 3 months. To serve, thaw in the refrigerator overnight. Reheat in a preheated 170°C (325°F) mark 3 oven for 10 to 15 minutes before serving.

12.   Bake the remaining 24 triangles following the same method.

Makes 48 triangles.

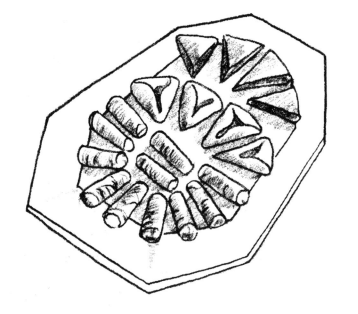

Spinach and Cheese Omelette

This spinach and onion blend, seasoned with ricotta and feta cheeses, also makes an excellent filling for a breakfast or luncheon omelette. Serve it topped with a dollop of yogurt.

FLUTED PITA MEAT PIES

The aroma wafting its way from the oven as these savoury pies bake to a turn is enough to tempt even the most disciplined dieter! Circles of Basic Pita dough are rolled then topped with a spicy blend of minced lamb, tomatoes, parsley, and cayenne, and closed to a fluted perfection. Serve them piping hot from the oven as appetizers with Taratour (Sesame and Garlic Sauce). While you're at it, freeze a batch for make-ahead convenience! What a treat unexpected guests have in store! Vary these fluted dainties the next time around by using the minced lamb, cinnamon, and yogurt filling in Pita Pyramids, page 66.

900 g (2 lb) minced lean lamb or beef
1 large onion, finely chopped
3 large fresh tomatoes, skinned, seeded, chopped, and squeezed to remove as much liquid as possible; or one 800 g (1 lb 12 oz) can tomatoes, drained, squeezed and mashed
105 ml (7 tbsp) tomato ketchup
15 ml (1 tbsp) finely chopped fresh parsley
Salt and freshly ground black pepper, to taste
Pinch of cayenne
1 recipe Basic Pita dough, page 21, prepared up to step 2
100 ml (4 fl oz) clarified butter, melted, page 56
Taratour (sesame and garlic sauce; recipe follows)

1. Combine the meat, onion, tomatoes, tomato ketchup, parsley, salt, pepper, and cayenne in a medium bowl. Mix thoroughly. Refrigerate, covered, to chill.

2. Divide the pita dough into 48 portions. Shape each portion into a smooth ball. Place on a floured work surface and cover with slightly damp tea-towels to keep the surface of the dough supple and moist. Let rest 30 to 45 minutes in a warm, draught-free place.

3. Place 1 rack near the bottom third of the oven and another one just above it. Preheat the oven to 220°C (425°F) mark 7. Lightly grease 2 baking sheets.

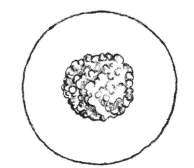

Centre filling on dough.

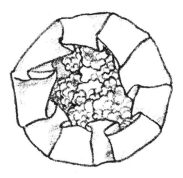

Bring up the dough edge, and use your fingers, to make tucks around the pie.

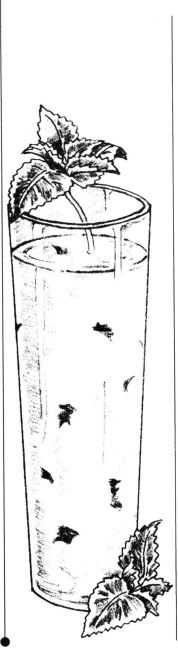

4. Working in 2 batches of 24 pies at a time, gently press each ball flat with your fingers, keeping it well rounded. Flour a work surface and rolling pin. Roll each round of dough into an 8.5 cm (3½ inch) circle.

5. Divide the meat mixture equally into 48 portions, about 1 rounded tablespoon each, and place 1 portion in the centre of each circle. Flute the sides by bringing folds to within 2.5 cm (1 inch) of the centre. See illustration on page 63. Press the fluted edges down firmly.

6. Arrange 12 pies on each of the 2 greased baking sheets. Lightly brush with clarified butter.

7. Bake 2 sheets at a time, placing 1 sheet on each pre-positioned oven rack staggering 1 on the right and 1 on the left. Reverse the sheets from the top to bottom racks halfway through baking for even heat distribution. Bake until lightly browned, 20 to 25 minutes.

8. Repeat the process with the remaining 24 rounds of dough and the meat mixture while the first batch bakes.

9. Remove the baked pies from the oven and brush again with clarified butter. Serve immediately or cool on wire racks and refrigerate, covered, for up to 3 days or freeze for up to 3 months. To serve, thaw in the refrigerator overnight. Reheat in a preheated 170°C (325°F) mark 3 oven for 10 to 15 minutes before serving.

10. Bake the remaining 24 pies following the same method.

Makes 48.

LEMONADE WITH ORANGE-BLOSSOM WATER

As a child, I recall my mother served this tall cool glass of "heaven" to her church circle group. When I was old enough to start cooking, I found out its secret ingredient was orange-blossom water!

75 ml (3 fl oz) fresh lemon juice
475 ml (16 fl oz) ice water
2.5–5 ml (½–1 tsp) orange-blossom
    water, to taste

Sugar, to taste
Ice
Lemon slices (garnish)
Fresh mint sprigs (garnish)

Combine the lemon juice, ice water, orange-blossom water, and sugar in a jug. Blend well. Pour into ice-filled glasses. Garnish with lemon slices and mint sprigs.

Makes 2 to 3 servings.

TARATOUR
(Sesame and Garlic Sauce)

Throughout the Middle East, this classic sauce appears in many forms and with numerous subtle variations in seasonings. Basically a mixture of Tahini (sesame seed paste), garlic, lemon juice, salt, and pepper, it is used as a sauce for steamed or fried vegetables, a dip for crudités or pita crisps, and thinned, as a salad dressing or topping for pita sandwiches.

275 g (10 oz) Tahini (sesame seed paste), page 41
2 cloves garlic, crushed
90 ml (6 tbsp) fresh lemon juice
Salt and freshly ground black pepper, to taste
60–100 ml (2–4 fl oz) water
Chopped fresh parsley (garnish)

1.   Combine the tahini, garlic, lemon juice, salt, and pepper in a bowl or blender. Mix or blend until smooth.

2.   Gradually add the water until the sauce reaches the desired consistency. The dip should be thicker than a dressing or sauce. Taste to correct seasonings. Pour into a medium bowl. Garnish with the chopped parsley.

Makes about 450 ml (¾ pint).

A Middle Eastern Sunday Supper

Hot Hummus and Feta Cheese with Sesame Pita Crisps/ Wholemeal Honey Pita wedges
Pita Pyramids
Middle-Eastern Meatballs with Basic Pitas
Cucumber and Yogurt Salad
Glazed Pita Puffs
Spiced Turkish Coffee

PITA PYRAMIDS
(Fatayer)

Every country has its own version of meat pies or turnovers. *Fatayer* belongs to the Arab world. They may be round and fluted, rolled, turned over, or, as we've done here, shaped into a pyramid or triangle. Pita dough is a chewy natural wrap for these tart and tangy fillings of minced lamb or beef, cinnamon, yogurt, and pine nuts. Make the pies soft and buttery by brushing them with clarified butter as they come piping hot from the oven.

900 g (2 lb) minced lean lamb or beef
1 large onion, finely chopped
100 ml (4 fl oz) natural yogurt, preferably homemade, page 32
1.25 ml (¼ tsp) ground cinnamon
Salt and freshly ground black pepper, to taste
50 g (2 oz) pine nuts
1 recipe Basic Pita dough, page 21, prepared up to step 2
120 ml (8 tbsp) clarified butter, melted, page 56
Yogurt-Garlic Sauce, page 52

1. Combine the meat, onion, yogurt, cinnamon, salt, pepper, and pine nuts in a medium bowl. Mix thoroughly. Refrigerate, covered, to chill.

2. Divide the pita dough into 48 portions. Shape each portion into a smooth ball. Place on a floured work surface and cover with slightly damp tea-towels to keep the surface of the dough supple and moist. Let rest 30 to 45 minutes in a warm draught-free place.

3. Place 1 rack near the bottom third of the oven and another one just above it. Preheat the oven to 220°C (425°F) mark 7. Lightly grease 2 baking sheets.

4. Working in 2 batches of 24 pies at a time, gently press each ball flat with your fingers, keeping it well rounded. Flour a work surface and a rolling pin. Roll each round of dough into an 8.5 cm (3½ inch) circle.

5. Divide the meat mixture equally into 48 portions, about 1 rounded tablespoon each, and place 1 portion in the centre of each circle. Pick up the edges and pinch 3 sides of each circle firmly together, leaving a small opening in the centre, to form a triangle. See illustration on opposite page.

6. Arrange 12 pies on each of the 2 greased baking sheets. Lightly brush with clarified butter. Press the tops slightly to close the edges securely.

7. Bake 2 sheets at a time, placing 1 sheet on each pre-positioned oven rack staggering 1 on the right and 1 on the left. Reverse the sheets from the top to bottom racks halfway through baking for even heat distribution. Bake until lightly browned, 20 to 25 minutes.

8. Repeat the process with the remaining 24 rounds of dough and the meat mixture while the first batch bakes.

9. Remove the baked pies from the oven and brush again with clarified butter. Serve immediately or cool on wire racks and refrigerate, covered, for up to 3 days or freeze for up to 3 months. To serve, thaw in the refrigerator overnight. Reheat in a preheated 170°C (325°F) mark 3 oven until warmed through, about 15 minutes.

10. Bake the remaining 24 pies, following the same method.

Makes 48.

Tip

For dinner-sized servings, divide the dough into 24 equal portions and roll each into a 12.5 or 15 cm (5 or 6 inch) circle. Divide the filling evenly among the 24 pies and close. Makes 2 dozen large pies.

Centre filling on dough.

Pinch up two-thirds of the dough edge. Then bring up the third.

For pyramids leave a small opening at the top. For triangles, seal the seams tightly.

COURGETTE PATTIES WITH YOGURT-GARLIC SAUCE

These unusual patties, first cousins to potato pancakes, are especially good topped with a dollop of Yogurt-Garlic Sauce.

225 g (8 oz) courgettes, grated
Salt
2 eggs, beaten
1 small onion, minced
Freshly ground black pepper, to
*   taste*
About 65 g (2½ oz) plain white flour
Vegetable oil, for frying
Yogurt-Garlic Sauce, page 52
Sesame Pitas, page 22, cut into
*   wedges*

1.   Place the courgettes in a colander set over a medium bowl. Sprinkle lightly with salt and toss to mix. Set aside for 30 minutes. Squeeze out the water. Pat the courgettes dry on kitchen paper.

2.   Return the courgettes to the bowl and add the eggs, onion, and pepper, and stir to blend. Gradually add up to 65 g (2½ oz) flour, stirring, to bind the mixture. Divide into 12 patties.

3.   Pour the oil to a depth of 0.5 cm (¼ inch) in a frying pan and heat until hot but not smoking. Working in batches, add the patties and fry over medium heat, turning once, until golden-brown, about 2 minutes. Remove with a slotted spoon and drain on kitchen paper. Add more oil, if necessary, for subsequent batches.

4.   Serve the courgette patties drizzled with the yogurt-garlic sauce and surrounded by freshly made sesame pita wedges.

Makes 12 patties.

FRIED AUBERGINE AND COURGETTE WITH TARATOUR

Easy to make and delectable, these are a great addition to the *meze* spread.

1 small aubergine, peeled, halved
    lengthwise, and cut into
    0.5 cm (¼ inch) slices
3 medium courgettes (about 5 cm/
    2 inches in diameter), peeled,
    halved lengthwise, and cut into
    0.5 cm (¼ inch) slices
Salt
Vegetable oil, for frying
Taratour (sesame and garlic sauce),
    page 65
Basic Pitas, page 21, cut into wedges

1. Lightly salt both sides of the aubergine and courgette slices. Layer them on kitchen paper and cover the top with another layer of kitchen paper. Set aside for 1 hour to drain off excess moisture. Pat dry with fresh kitchen paper.

2. Pour the oil to a depth of 0.5 cm (¼ inch) in a frying pan and heat until hot but not smoking. Working in batches, add the aubergine and courgettes and fry over medium heat until golden-brown, 2 to 3 minutes. Remove with a slotted spoon and drain on kitchen paper. Add more oil, if necessary, for subsequent batches.

3. Arrange the aubergine and courgette slices on a serving platter and lace with taratour (sesame and garlic sauce). Surround with pita wedges and offer a bowl of additional sauce for those who may want more.

Makes 6 to 8 servings.

Tip

Both courgette patties and fried aubergine and courgette slices also make wonderful pita sandwiches when laced with yogurt-garlic sauce or taratour and topped with shredded Cos lettuce.

HOT BON CHAMPIGNON BRIE ON DUXELLES

Mushroom duxelles, that dry, delicious mushroom flavouring, used generously by French chefs for many kinds of stuffings and sauces, makes a wonderful base for Bon Champignon cheese-stuffed pitas. This is a great way to use up leftover pieces of plain brie, even though I've suggested using the mushroom brie as a starter. I like the "double-champignon" flavour. And if you don't make the duxelles, mushroom brie used alone is super!

Medium Basic Pitas, page 21, split into rounds
1 recipe Duxelles (recipe follows)
Mushroom Brie, sliced into 0.3–0.5 cm (⅛–¼ inch) wedges

1. Preheat the grill.

2. Lightly spread the bottom rounds of the pitas with a layer of duxelles. Top with slices of mushroom brie and place on a baking sheet. Grill until hot and bubbly, about 5 minutes.

3. Place the pita top on the hot brie and bake in a preheated oven until the top is warm, 1 to 2 minutes.

4. Slice into wedges with a serrated knife and serve immediately.

Duxelles

450 g (1 lb) fresh mushrooms, wiped clean with damp kitchen paper and finely minced
50 g (2 oz) butter
30 ml (2 tbsp) vegetable oil
4 medium shallots, minced
Salt and freshly ground black pepper, to taste
100 ml (4 fl oz) dry white wine

1. Working in batches over a bowl, squeeze small scoops of the mushrooms into tight balls in kitchen paper to remove as much liquid as possible; reserve the liquid.

2. Melt the butter in the oil in a frying pan. Add the mushrooms and shallots and sauté over medium heat, stirring frequently, until they begin to dry out and brown, about 10 to 12 minutes. Season with salt and pepper to taste.

3. Add the wine and reserved mushroom liquid and continue to cook over medium-high heat until all the liquid has evaporated. Cool and use as desired. To store, refrigerate, covered, for up to 1 week or freeze for up to 3 months.

Makes about 350 g (12 oz).

GINGERED FIG MONTRACHET

Since early times, figs have been revered by the Hebrews as a reflection of peace and plenty. Today both green and purple figs are plumper and sweeter than ever, thanks to modern-day cultivation. To prove it, we've combined fresh purple figs and minced ginger with softened Montrachet to make a delightful goat cheese spread. Offer crunchy pita crisps and serve a dry white wine or a spiced herbal tea to accompany this elegant offering.

350 g (12 oz) goat cheese (such as Montrachet)
30–60 ml (2–4 tbsp) single cream
3 to 4 purple figs, finely chopped
5 ml (1 tsp) finely minced fresh ginger
15 ml (1 tbsp) fresh lemon juice, to taste
Freshly ground black pepper, to taste
Sweet Sesame Pita Crisps, page 28

1. Break up the log of Montrachet and place in a blender or food processor fitted with the metal blade. With the machine running, add the single cream in a thin steady stream. Process until the mixture is creamy and spreadable.

2. Transfer the cheese mixture to a medium bowl and add the remaining ingredients except the pita crisps. Mix gently until well blended. Refrigerate, covered, to chill.

3. Transfer the spread to a serving bowl. Offer with sweet sesame pita crisps.

Makes about 450 g (1 lb).

Sunny Sunday Brunch

Orange-blossom Screwdrivers
Fresh melon slices with pomegranate garnish
Hot Bon Champignon Brie on Duxelles in a Pita
Classic Parsley and Onion Omelette Wedges in buttered Basic Pita wedges
Spinach and Feta Triangles
Coriander and Lamb Sausage Patties wrapped in Griddle-Baked Pitas
Spiced Glazed Figs with Hazelnuts and Sweetened Sesame Pitas
Coffee or Tea

FRIED LEMON-LACED CHEESE

A lacing of lemon juice gives a classic fried-cheese appetizer an entirely new and lively personality. To give the cheese cubes more body when they are fried, chill them, uncovered, in the refrigerator for several hours. They are particularly tasty when wrapped in Griddle-Baked Pitas and served with apple wedges, grapes, or fresh white figs, and a bottle of your favourite white wine.

450 g (1 lb) hard, dry cheese, such as
    Cheddar
1 large clove garlic, cut in half
65 g (2½ oz) plain white flour
2.5 ml (½ tsp) crumbled dried thyme
60 ml (4 tbsp) vegetable oil
30 ml (2 tbsp) fresh lemon juice
Lemon wedges (garnish)
Griddle-Baked Pitas, page 31

1. Rub the cheese with the cut garlic, then cut into 4 cm (1½ inch) cubes. Refrigerate to chill.

2. Combine the flour and thyme in a small bowl. Blend thoroughly. Dredge the cheese cubes in the flour.

3. Heat the oil in a frying pan until it is hot but not smoking. Add the coated cubes, and fry, over medium-high heat, turning frequently, until brown on all sides but not melted, about 1½ to 2 minutes.

4. Place the cheese on a warm serving platter and lace with the lemon juice. Garnish with lemon wedges and serve immediately. Surround with griddle-baked pitas which guests may use to wrap around these delicate morsels.

Makes 6 to 8 servings.

BASIL FONDUE PIEDMONTESE

This is a Middle Eastern version of the famous Fondue Piedmontese. Instead of surrounding the cheese fondue with sautéed slices of Italian bread, I've used Pita Crisps. And instead of garnishing the fondue with truffles, I've opted for the less expensive but delicious black Greek olives.

100 g (4 oz) Fontina cheese, diced, or 100 g (4 oz) mozzarella, diced
25 g (1 oz) grated Gruyère cheese
15 ml (1 tbsp) cornflour
175 ml (6 fl oz) milk
1 egg yolk
15 ml (1 tbsp) finely chopped fresh basil
15 ml (1 tbsp) sliced black Greek olives (garnish)
Savoury Pita Crisps, page 28

1. Put the diced and grated cheeses into the top of a double boiler.

2. Blend the cornflour with the milk and egg yolk. Add to the cheeses.

3. Add the basil and stir the cheese-milk mixture over simmering water until completely melted and smooth. Pour into a heated serving bowl or fondue dish. Garnish with the olives and surround with a variety of savoury pita crisps. Serve immediately.

Makes about 450 g (1 lb).

WALNUT-STUFFED VINE LEAVES

Vegetables and nut-stuffed vine leaves cooked in olive oil and lemon juice are a variation of meat-stuffed vine leaves adapted originally by families observing the meatless Lenten season. Today these tart yet sweetish delicacies are a popular appetizer accompanied by soft pita. Serve them at room temperature to bring out the flavours.

two 225 g (8 oz) packets vine leaves (50 to 60 leaves)
100 ml (4 fl oz) olive oil, plus oil for drizzling
1 large onion, finely chopped
200 g (7 oz) long-grain rice
50 g (2 oz) chopped walnuts
50 g (2 oz) sultanas
10 ml (2 tsp) chopped fresh dill
1.25 ml (¼ tsp) ground cinnamon
Salt and freshly ground black pepper, to taste
100 ml (4 fl oz) fresh lemon juice
450–600 ml (¾–1 pint) boiling water
Lemon wedges
Wholemeal Honey Pitas, page 23, cut into wedges

1. Drain the vine leaves and soak them in cold water for about 30 minutes. Drain and rinse them again until all the salt is removed then squeeze them gently to remove excess moisture. Cut off the stems and set aside.

2. Heat 100 ml (4 fl oz) of olive oil in a frying pan. Add the onions and sauté over medium heat until soft and transparent, about 5 minutes. Add the rice and toss to coat with the oil. Add the walnuts, sultanas, dill, cinnamon, salt, and pepper. Taste to correct seasonings. Remove from the heat and let cool.

3. Drizzle the bottom of a large, deep pan with olive oil and line it with a single layer of vine leaves.

4. To stuff the remaining leaves, place each leaf, vein-side up, on a plate or cutting board. Spoon about 15 ml (1 tbsp) of the rice mixture in the centre of each leaf. Tuck the bottom of the leaf over the filling, fold the sides over the centre, and roll up into a tight, neat packet. Stack the stuffed vine leaves, folded-side down, in a single layer in the pan. Arrange a second layer at right angles to the first. See illustration.

5. Mix the lemon juice with at least 450 ml (¾ pint) of boiling water and pour over the vine leaves. Invert a heat-proof plate over the layers to hold them in place during cooking. Add more boiling water (up to 100 ml (4 fl oz)), if necessary, to reach the top of the inverted plate. Cover and simmer over medium-low heat until the rice is tender to the bite, about 45 minutes. Drain the liquid and cool.

6. Serve at room temperature garnished with lemon wedges. Offer guests a basket of basic pita wedges to mop up the lemony liquid.

Makes about 50 to 60 stuffed vine leaves.

Variation *Tabbouleh-Stuffed Vine Leaves:* Stuff each vine leaf with 15 ml (1 tbsp) of tabbouleh (page 98) and cook as above.

Fluffy Rice? Add Lemon!

For stuffed vine or cabbage leaves or any stuffing mixtures, add 15 ml (1 tbsp) of fresh lemon juice to each 200 g (7 oz) of rice. This will ensure fluffy, tender, separate grains of rice every time.

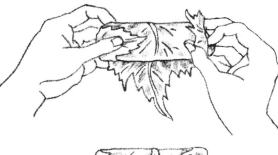

Centre filling on leaf.

Tuck the bottom of the leaf over filling.

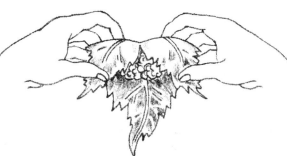

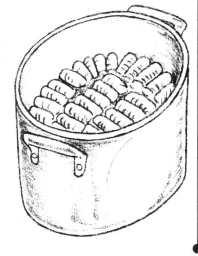

Fold sides towards the centre and continue rolling into a tight packet.

OLIVE PASTE TARTS WITH YOGURT CHEESE

Here, toasted pita rounds are topped with Fresh Yogurt Cheese then spread with a tangy olive paste and sprinkled with dried mint. This olive paste is similar to a traditional French tapenade, minus the anchovies which seem to overpower the distinctive flavour of the capers. This makes an excellent appetizer or an unusual breakfast spread when served with pita toast.

250 g (9 oz) black Greek olives, pitted
30 ml (2 tbsp) capers, drained
1 clove garlic, sliced
15 ml (1 tbsp) fresh lemon juice
2.5–5 ml (½–1 tsp) Dijon mustard, to taste
Freshly ground black pepper, to taste
15 ml (1 tbsp) white wine
60–120 ml (4–8 tbsp) olive oil
Small Basic Pitas, page 21, split into rounds and toasted
Yogurt Cheese, page 33

1. Combine the olives, capers, garlic, lemon juice, mustard, pepper, and white wine in a blender or food processor fitted with the metal blade and process until smooth.

2. With the machine running, add enough oil in a thin, steady stream to make a thick, smooth, spreadable paste. Taste to correct seasonings. Refrigerate, covered, to chill.

3. Spread the cooled, toasted pita rounds with the yogurt cheese. Top with a thin layer of the olive paste and serve as an appetizer or a breakfast spread.

Makes about 350 g (12 oz).

Music-In-The-Park Supper

Champagne
Olive-Paste Tarts with Basic Pitas
Chicken Salad Béarnaise with Wholemeal Sesame Pitas
Market Salad with Basilica Vinaigrette
Spiced Glazed Figs with Hazelnuts
Spiced Turkish Coffee

OPEN-FACED GOAT CHEESE PITA TARTS

These savoury tarts are made from a hard goat cheese that has been marinated in a vegetable broth laced with Cognac, then blended until smooth. Serve them hot straight from the grill. Any remaining spread makes a great dip served with Garlic Pita Crisps.

300 ml (½ pint) water
50 g (2 oz) chopped leeks, both white
    and green
15 g (½ oz) snipped fresh chives or
    45 ml (3 tbsp) dried chives
15 ml (1 tbsp) finely chopped shallot
1 small bay leaf
22 ml (1½ tbsp) Cognac
1.25 ml (¼ tsp) crumbled dried
    thyme
5 ml (1 tsp) chopped fresh tarragon
350 g (12 oz) goat cheese—such as
    Crottin de Chavignol
Small Basic Pitas, page 21, split
    into rounds and toasted

1.   Twenty-four hours before serving, combine all the ingredients except for 2.5 ml (½ tsp) of the tarragon, the cheese, and the pita in a medium saucepan. Bring to a boil, then reduce the heat and simmer, covered, for 30 minutes. Cool the broth to lukewarm and strain. Put the cheese and vegetable broth in an earthenware crock or glass bowl. Cover and refrigerate for 24 hours.

2.   Preheat the grill.

3.   Place the cheese and broth in a blender or food processor fitted with the metal blade and process until smooth. Add more water or additional cheese if necessary to achieve a spreadable paste.

4.   Spread the toasted pita rounds with the goat-cheese mixture and top with the remaining tarragon. Grill until warm and bubbly. Serve immediately.

Makes about 450 g (1 lb) goat-cheese spread.

FRESH PITA PIZZA

Make a super pizza out of the Basic Pita dough—it is quite like the dough used for pizzas. Try it with a variety of fresh vegetables layered on top of mounds of shredded mozzarella. You can be sure that this pizza will star as an appetizer or weekend snack.

Basic Pizza

½ recipe Basic Pita dough, page 21, prepared up to step 2
60 ml (2 tbsp) olive oil
225 g (8 oz) mozzarella cheese, grated
Salt and freshly ground black pepper, to taste
Pizza toppings (see below)
15 g (½ oz) chopped fresh coriander
30 ml (2 tbsp) grated Parmesan

Pizza Toppings

Lightly fried aubergine slices
Lightly fried courgette slices
Chopped fresh tomato
Sliced green or red pepper
Sliced and sautéed fresh mushrooms
Lamb, onion, and pine nut sauté (filling used for Stuffed Kibbeh, page 56)
Pitted and sliced black Greek olives

1. Divide the dough into 2 portions. Shape each portion into a smooth ball. Place on a floured work surface and cover with slightly damp tea-towels. Let rest in a warm draught-free place, 30 to 45 minutes.

2. Place a rack in the lowest position in the oven. Preheat the oven to 230°C (450°F) mark 8. Lightly grease two 25.5 or 30.5 cm (10 or 12 inch) pizza pans or baking sheets.

3. Preparing 1 pizza at a time, gently press each ball flat with your fingers, keeping it well rounded. Flour a work surface and rolling pin. Roll the round of dough into a 25.5 or 30.5 cm (10 or 12 inch) circle, pulling at the edges with your fingers and turning several times until you reach the desired size. Gently place the circle on a pizza pan or baking sheet. Pinch the edges up slightly to form a ridge. Drizzle the circle with 30 ml (2 tbsp) of olive oil and spread it to the rim.

4. Cover the pizza with 100 g (4 oz) grated mozzarella. Add salt, pepper, and a combination of toppings. Sprinkle with 30 ml (2 tbsp) coriander and 15 ml (1 tbsp) of grated Parmesan.

5. Bake until the crust is golden brown, 15 to 20 minutes. Remove from the oven.

6. Repeat the process with the second pizza.

7. Cut the wedges with a pizza cutter and serve immediately.

Makes two 25.5 or 30.5 cm (10 or 12 inch) pizzas.

MARINATED ARTICHOKES WITH PEPPERS

For a unique and different appetizer, try this medley of artichokes, black Greek olives, and peppers. The lustiness of the olives and the hot peppers perfectly complement the delicate artichokes.

two 200 g (7 oz) cans artichoke hearts, drained
75–115 g (3–4½ oz) black Greek olives
12 red or green peppers preserved in vinegar
60 ml (4 tbsp) olive oil
15 ml (1 tbsp) red wine vinegar
30 ml (2 tbsp) fresh lemon juice
2 spring onions, finely chopped
Salt and freshly ground black pepper, to taste
Finely chopped fresh coriander (garnish)
Wheat-Germ Honey Pitas, page 24, cut into wedges

1. Combine the artichoke hearts, olives, and peppers in a medium bowl.

2. Blend the olive oil, vinegar, lemon juice, onions, salt, and pepper in a small bowl. Taste to correct seasonings. Add the dressing to the salad mixture and toss to coat. Refrigerate, covered, for at least 2 hours or overnight.

3. Drain and discard the dressing. Serve the salad on a platter. Garnish with the coriander. Serve wheat-germ honey pita wedges on the side.

Makes 6 appetizer servings.

ANTIPASTO PITA

Fill a Wholemeal Honey Pita with Genoa salami, cervalat, or pepperoni. Top with Homemade Roasted Peppers, page 80, chickpeas, sliced tomatoes, red onions, and mozzarella. Drizzle a little marinade from the roasted peppers over everything and garnish with chopped fresh basil leaves and pitted black Greek olives.

HOMEMADE ROASTED PEPPERS

Fresh sweet red peppers, roasted and charred to a soft perfection, are ideal for spicing up many salad fillings to stuff in a pita. They are also super additions to a charcuterie board or a Pita Antipasto spread, page 79.

8 medium (about 1.1 kg/2½ lb) red peppers
75 ml (3 fl oz) olive oil
45 ml (3 tbsp) red wine vinegar
50 g (2 oz) chopped spring onions
Salt and freshly ground black pepper, to taste
1 clove garlic, cut in half

1. Preheat the oven to 230°C (450°F) mark 8.

2. Wash and drain the peppers and place on a baking sheet. Bake, turning them about every 5 minutes, until the skins are charred and blistered, about 20 to 25 minutes.

3. Immediately transfer the peppers to a brown paper bag and close tightly. Let stand until the peppers are cool and the skins have begun to separate from the flesh, about 20 to 30 minutes.

4. Peel off the skins, using a knife if necessary. Seed the peppers and remove the membranes. Cut into bite-sized pieces.

5. Blend the olive oil, vinegar, onions, salt, pepper, and garlic in a large bowl. Taste to correct seasonings. Add the peppers and toss gently to coat. Cover and marinate, in the refrigerator, turning occasionally, for at least 3 hours.

6. Serve at room temperature as a condiment with pita sandwiches, charcuterie, or a pita antipasto spread. To store, refrigerate, covered, for up to 1 week.

Makes about 900 g (2 lb).

PIQUANT PICKLED TURNIPS
(Lif-fit)

Piquant pink pickled turnips, called *Lif-fit* in Arabic, are classic Middle Eastern condiments served before or during a meal and always accompanied by pita, of course. These appetizer pickles get their pretty colour by the addition of beetroot and beetroot juice to the pickling solution. Every time I share this recipe with friends, it becomes a part of their permanent culinary repertoire. Remember, though, that it takes three days to pickle the turnips, so plan ahead.

1.1–1.4 kg (2½–3 lb) medium white turnips
Salt
450 g (1 lb) small whole beetroots, cooked, peeled, and juice reserved or 326 g (11½ oz) jar small whole beetroots drained and juice reserved
Black peppercorns
350 ml (12 fl oz) lukewarm water
350 ml (12 fl oz) white vinegar
10 ml (2 tsp) salt or to taste

1. Three days before serving, wash the unpeeled turnips and slice off the tops and bottoms. Remove any brown spots with a vegetable brush or scrape lightly with a knife. Cut into halves, if small, or in quarters if large and place in a large bowl. Lightly salt and set aside at room temperature for 6 to 8 hours, frequently draining off excess water.

2. Place the turnips in 2 sterilized 900 g (2 lb) glass jars. Add at least 2 beetroots and several peppercorns to each jar.

3. Combine the water, vinegar, salt, and 100 ml (4 fl oz) reserved beetroot juice in a bowl. Pour over the turnips, leaving 1 cm (½ inch) of space at the top (if you fill the jars to the top, the liquid may leak as the turnips begin their fermentation).

4. Seal and set aside in a cool place for three days to expedite the pickling process before refrigerating. Turn the jars upside down occasionally so the colour is dispersed throughout and the top turnips are evenly coated and exposed to the pickling solution. Refrigerate after the third day.

Makes 1.8 kg (4 lb).

Tip

Easy appetizers that complement pita include:
- Marinated olives
- Fresh dates stuffed with unsalted Yogurt Cheese
- Sliced tomatoes sprinkled with fresh coriander or basil and freshly ground black pepper
- Cold prawns or diced avocado marinated in olive oil, lemon juice, crushed garlic, salt, and freshly ground black pepper.

MARINATED BLACK GREEK OLIVES

Olives are always a part of a Middle Eastern *meze* spread. The choices are many although we prefer the Calamata variety since they are especially assertive in flavour and appearance. They are sold in brine, loose or packed in containers, and while they may be eaten as purchased, it is a good idea to marinate them first to subdue their saltiness and soften the flavour.

Soak the olives in cold water then drain them, repeating this process several times over a period of 2 to 3 hours or overnight to remove the excess brine. Taste them to test the flavour. Place 900 g (2 lb) of olives in a clean jar and drizzle 15 ml (1 tbsp) of olive oil and 5 ml (1 tsp) of wine vinegar over the top. Cover and turn the jar upside down several times to coat the olives.

Refrigerate to help retain the flavour. Before serving, set them out at room temperature and repeat the upside-down blending once more to coat the olives. This small amount of marinade gives them just a hint of flavour and adds an appetizing shimmer. You may use more olive oil and vinegar, if desired, though we find this proportion above is just enough to season and coat the olives yet keep them firm.

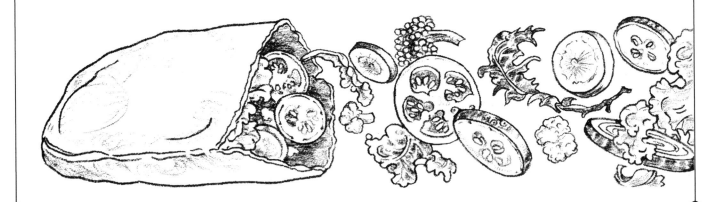

CAULIFLOWER AND ONION PICKLES

(Quarnabeet Bi Busil)

These tart cauliflower and onion pickles, called *Quarnabeet Bi Busil* in Arabic, are a popular pre-dinner appetizer at a Mediterranean meal. I've broken from classic tradition to include button onions as a crunchy team-mate. Usually served with an assortment of other condiments, these pickles seem to be the first to go! Chopped and coated with a light drizzle of Taratour (sesame and garlic sauce), they also make a delightful topping for a *Falafel* or *Kibbeh* sandwich.

1 medium (about 1.1 kg/2½ lb) cauliflower separated into florets and parboiled
225 g (8 oz) button onions, about 2.5–4 cm (1–1½ inches) in diameter, parboiled
450 g (1 lb) small whole beetroots, cooked, peeled, and juice reserved or 326 g (11½ oz) jar small whole beetroots, drained and juice reserved
Black peppercorns
350 ml (12 fl oz) lukewarm water
350 ml (12 fl oz) white vinegar
Salt to taste

1. Three days before serving, place the cauliflower and the onions in 2 sterilized 900 g (2 lb) glass jars. Add at least 2 beetroots and several peppercorns to each jar.

2. Combine the water, vinegar, salt, and 100 ml (4 fl oz) reserved beetroot juice in a bowl. Pour over the cauliflower and onions, leaving 1 cm (½ inch) of space at the top (if you fill the jars to the top, the liquid may leak as the cauliflower and onions begin their fermentation).

3. Seal and set aside in a cool place for three days to expedite the pickling process before refrigerating. Turn the jars upside down occasionally so the colour is dispersed throughout and the top pickles are evenly coated and exposed to the pickling solution. Refrigerate after the third day.

Makes 1.8 kg (4 lb).

PITA CHARCUTERIE

On a warm summer's evening, offer friends a Pita Charcuterie. Set out baskets full of soft fresh pitas, a tray of thinly sliced meats including fresh roast pork, smoked chicken, and rare roast beef, and a selection of pâtés and sausages. Condiments, of course, should abound—mild and spicy mustards, sweet and dill pickles, Marinated Black Greek Olives, page 82, Homemade Roasted Peppers, page 80, and Piquant Pickled Turnips, page 81.

PITA ALONGSIDES

Traditionally soups and salads are served as separate courses of an elaborate meal, but nowadays they can be a complete meal in themselves with lots of warm pitas for dunking and scooping.

The soups I have included are based on simple Middle Eastern peasant fare—yogurt, legumes, spinach, pasta, mint, lemon, garlic, and olive oil—all the foods that go so well with pita. There's even a soup that uses pita dough in the form of dumplings. Make these soups ahead to enhance their flavours and reduce last-minute work.

As for the salads, many will double as appetizers and as toppings for a pita-filled sandwich while others are meals in themselves or make great accompaniments to other dishes. Tomato and Onion Salad, for instance, is often served at the *meze* spread and *Kibbeh* (Middle-Eastern Meat-balls) stuffed into pitas and topped with Cucumber and Yogurt Salad make very tasty sandwiches. *Tabbouleh* can be served alongside so many of the dishes, while Chef's Couscous Salad, chock full of greens, bulgur, and tender slices of roast lamb and chicken, satisfies the appetite of the heartiest eater so long as there are plenty of pitas to scoop it all up, of course.

SPINACH AND LENTIL SOUP
(Addas Bi Hamoud)

This hearty potage of lentils and spinach, called *Addas Bi Hamoud* in Arabic and translated to mean a sour lentil soup or lentils with lemon, is a favourite in Middle Eastern homes. And you can bet it is always served with baskets full of warm pita. Make a double batch of this pita companion and freeze one for a cold winter's day. Serve it with Pita Bread Salad, page 101, for a hearty meal.

275 g (10 oz) lentils
2.3 litres (4 pints) water
15 ml (1 tbsp) salt
60 ml (4 tbsp) olive oil
1 large onion, chopped
1 clove garlic, crushed
2 medium potatoes, scrubbed, and diced with the skins left on (about 250 g/9 oz)
275 g (10 oz) fresh spinach, rinsed, patted dry, stems trimmed, and leaves torn into bite-sized pieces or one 300 g (10.6 oz) packet frozen leaf spinach
60 ml (4 tbsp) fresh lemon juice, or to taste
5 ml (1 tsp) ground coriander
Freshly ground black pepper, to taste
Wholemeal Sesame Pitas, page 24, cut into wedges.

1. Wash and drain the lentils. Put them in a large pan and add the water. Bring to a boil and add salt. Reduce the heat and simmer, covered, until the lentils are almost tender, 45 minutes to 1 hour.

2. Heat the oil in a frying pan. Add the onion and garlic and sauté over medium heat until soft and translucent, about 5 minutes.

3. Add the onion mixture to the lentils. Add the potatoes, spinach, 15 ml (1 tbsp) lemon juice, coriander, and pepper. If you are using frozen spinach, drop the frozen block into the hot lentil mixture and break up with a fork as it cooks. Stir thoroughly. Simmer covered, until the potatoes are tender, about 15 to 20 minutes. If the soup seems too thick, add a little boiling water to thin the mixture.

4. Just before serving, add the remaining lemon juice. Taste to correct seasonings. Serve accompanied with wedges of wholemeal sesame pita.

Makes 8 servings.

Picnic Pita Party

Spinach and Lentil Soup with Wholemeal Sesame Pitas
Grilled Kefta Kebabs in Sesame Pitas
Spicy Bulgur Salad
Feta Cheese and Cucumber Salad
Glazed Pita Puffs
Hearty Burgundy
Lots of Hot Coffee

NOODLES AND LENTIL HOT POT

(Rishta)

Called *Rishta* in Arabic, this rich peasant soup is a relative to the lemony Spinach and Lentil Soup and it, too, calls for stacks of warm pita for dunking. Noodles are the classic ingredient, but you might like to substitute new potatoes and even add other favourite vegetables such as carrots or swedes. Serve it alongside a dish of Minted Cabbage Salad.

400 g (14 oz) lentils
1.7 litres (3 pints) water
15 ml (1 tbsp) salt
75 ml (3 fl oz) olive oil
2 large onions, chopped
3 cloves garlic, finely chopped
75 g (3 oz) medium egg noodles
Freshly ground black pepper, to taste
Wheat-Germ Honey Pitas, page 24, cut into wedges

1. Wash and drain the lentils. Put them in a large pan and add the water. Bring to a boil and add the salt. Reduce the heat and simmer, covered, until the lentils are almost tender, 45 minutes to 1 hour.

2. Heat the oil in a frying pan. Add the onions and garlic, and sauté over medium heat until soft and translucent, about 5 minutes.

3. Add the onion mixture to the lentils. Add the noodles and pepper. Stir thoroughly. Simmer, covered, until the noodles are tender, about 20 to 25 minutes. If the soup seems too thick, add a little boiling water to thin the mixture. Taste to correct seasonings.

4. Serve accompanied with wedges of wheat-germ honey pita.

Makes 8 servings.

Vegetarian Supper

Courgette Patties with Yogurt-Garlic Sauce
Noodles and Lentil Hot Pot with Wheat-Germ Honey Pitas
Falafel topped with Chopped Vegetable Salad in Basic Pitas
Fresh pears and mozzarella with Sweet Sesame Pita Crisps
Cardamom Coffee

LITTLE PITA DUMPLINGS IN YOGURT SOUP

(Shish Barak Bi Laban)

This refreshingly delightful hot yogurt soup, dressed with garlic, melted butter, and fresh mint, shows off the tastiest little lamb and pine nut dumplings you've ever eaten. And conveniently, the dumplings are made with the same dough used to make Griddle-Baked Pita. With the dumpling-laden bowl of hot soup, chances are you won't need any bread, but I'll bet you can't resist a pita for dunking. Serve this accompanied by a crisp Classic Mediterranean Salad, page 94, and you've a memorable meal!

Pita Dumplings

350 g (12 oz) minced lean lamb
1 medium onion, finely chopped
1.25 ml (¼ tsp) ground cinnamon
Salt and freshly ground black
  pepper, to taste
40 g (1¼ oz) butter
½ recipe Griddle-Baked Pita,
  page 31, prepared up to step 2
25 g (1 oz) pine nuts

Yogurt Soup

1.7 litres (3 pints) yogurt preferably
  homemade, page 32
15 ml (1 tbsp) cornflour
1.1 litres (2 pints) cold water
1 egg, beaten
5 ml (1 tsp) salt
40 g (1½ oz) butter
1 large clove garlic, crushed
15 ml (1 tbsp) finely chopped fresh
  mint or 5 ml (1 tsp) crumbled
  dried mint
Basic Pitas, page 21, cut into wedges

1. To prepare the dumplings, combine the lamb, onion, cinnamon, salt and pepper in a small bowl. Melt the 40 g (1½ oz) of butter in a frying pan. Add the lamb mixture and cook over medium heat, breaking it up as it cooks, until all the pink colour has disappeared. Add the pine nuts and cook over high heat, stirring constantly, until lightly browned. Remove from the heat and let cool.

2. Divide the pita dough into 6 portions and shape into balls. Cover the balls with slightly damp tea-towels, and let rest about 5 to 10 minutes.

3. Press each ball flat with your fingers, keeping it well rounded. Flour a work surface and rolling pin. Roll out each round to form a circle 0.3 cm (⅛ inch) thick. With a biscuit cutter, cut the dough into 5 cm (2 inch) circles. Repeat the process with the remaining dough, gathering up and combining any scraps, until you have 36 circles. Any remaining dough can be made into griddle-baked pitas, according to the recipe, page 31.

4. Top each circle with a little of the lamb mixture, dividing it evenly among the 36 circles. Fold each circle in half and pinch the edges firmly together. Bring the ends together and press the corners. See illustration.

5. To prepare the soup, put the yogurt into a large saucepan and whisk until it is thinned and smooth. In a small bowl, dissolve the cornflour into 60 ml (4 tbsp) of the cold water, then whisk it into the yogurt. Whisk in the beaten egg and blend thoroughly. Whisk in the remaining water and salt. Bring to a boil over medium heat, stirring constantly. When the yogurt mixture is boiling, drop in the dumplings, reduce the heat and simmer, covered, stirring occasionally, until the dumplings are tender, about 25 to 30 minutes.

6. Melt the butter in a pan. Add the garlic and sauté over medium heat until softened and fragrant, about 3 minutes. Add to the soup. Stir in the mint and taste to correct seasonings. Serve immediately.

Makes 6 servings; 36 dumplings.

Variation *Yogurt Soup with Middle Eastern Meatballs:* In addition to or instead of Pita Dumplings, add walnut-size Kibbeh, page 51.

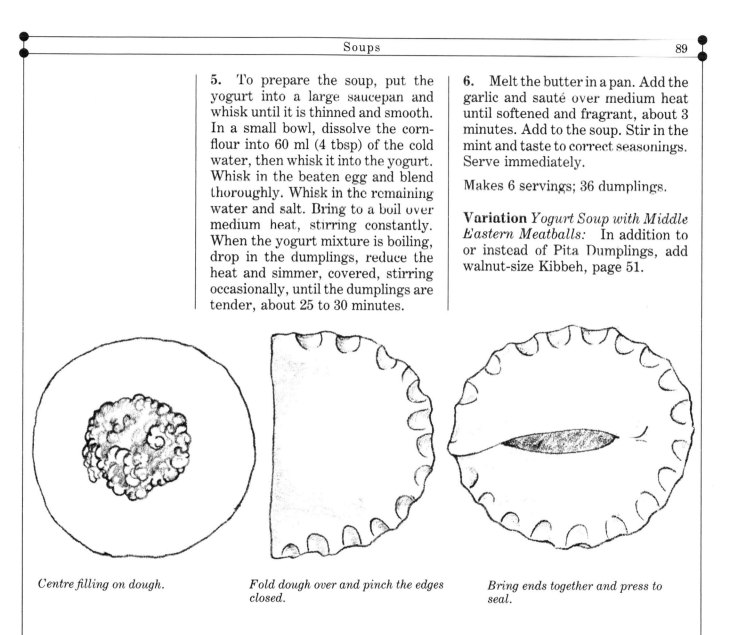

Centre filling on dough.

Fold dough over and pinch the edges closed.

Bring ends together and press to seal.

CHILLED CUCUMBER AND YOGURT SOUP

(Khyar Bi Laban)

Cucumbers and yogurt, seasoned with garlic and mint, appear in many forms throughout the East. Along the Mediterranean the combination is variously used as a sauce for dipping and lacing, as a salad dressing, and as a salad unto itself. In India, it is called raita and is served with curries as a topping or as an accompaniment. Here it stars as a zesty hot-weather soup to be served with garlicky Pita Crisps. Offer it as a first course to a Shish Kebab and pita meal, page 112. Always served icy cold, this soup can be made ahead and kept ready in the refrigerator.

1.7 litres (3 pints) yogurt, preferably homemade, page 32
4 medium cucumbers, peeled, seeded and drained
4 cloves garlic, crushed
Salt and freshly ground black pepper, to taste
22 ml (1½ tbsp) chopped fresh mint or 7.5 ml (1½ tsp) crumbled dried mint
50 g (2 oz) toasted pine nuts (garnish)
Garlic Pita Crisps, page 28

1. Put the yogurt into a large bowl and whisk until it is thinned and smooth.

2. Add the cucumbers, garlic, salt, pepper, and mint. Blend thoroughly. Taste to correct seasonings. Cover and refrigerate to chill.

3. Serve topped with a sprinkling of pine nuts, accompanied with garlic pita crisps.

Makes 8 servings.

SECRETS TO PREPARING SALAD AND SANDWICH GREENS

Salad greens play an important role in pita sandwiches and salads and should always be fresh and crisp. Greens make perfect liners for pita pockets and when shredded, offer a crunchy topping or serve as a base to catch a sauce or dressing.

The choice is wide in the market today: chicory, coriander, endive, parsley, radicchio, cabbage, spinach, watercress, and the lettuces: Cos, Iceberg, round and Webbs Wonder. Remember these few guidelines to their successful use:

• Wash and dry salad greens immediately after purchasing and refrigerate them as quickly as possible to ensure the retention of a crisp texture, pleasing colour, and good flavour.

• Drain all greens after washing them, shaking off as much water as possible, then blot them dry with kitchen paper.

• Store the washed greens in a vegetable crisper in the refrigerator. If you plan to store them for an extended period wrap them in dry kitchen paper, then place them in plastic bags.

• Remove bruised outer leaves on any head of lettuce. Leave the root ends on greens such as chicory, and Cos lettuce, and wash them thoroughly under running cold water.

• Greens with small leaves like coriander, parsley, and watercress are best stored in tightly covered jars or plastic bags.

• Remove cleaned, crisped salad greens from the refrigerator about 1 hour before using and tear them into bite-sized pieces. Tear the leaves gently to prevent them from discolouring. Return them to the refrigerator until serving time.

• Use dressing sparingly. Too much will make a salad wilt. I have given specific measurements for dressing ingredients in proportion to salad ingredients opting for lesser rather than greater amounts. On those occasions when you want to create a salad from scratch without a recipe, use 60 ml (4 tbsp) of dressing for each 700g (1½ lb) of greens. Toss gently, just until all the leaves are coated, not dripping. Once the salad is served, there should be no more than 5 ml (1 tsp) of dressing left in the bowl.

CAULIFLOWER, BROCCOLI, AND PEPPER SALAD

Parboiled, yet crisp-tender cauliflower and broccoli florets teamed with strips of bright yellow and red peppers are laced with a Tahini dressing that has been delicately seasoned with garlic and generous squeezings of lemon juice. Serve this sophisticated combination with warm Sesame Pita wedges.

½ small head (about 225g/8 oz) cauliflower, leaves trimmed, core removed, and cut into florets, parboiled, and drained.
225 g (8 oz) broccoli, tops cut into florets, parboiled, and drained
1 small yellow pepper, cored, seeded and thinly sliced
1 small red pepper, cored, seeded and thinly sliced
1 clove garlic, crushed
60 ml (4 tbsp) Tahini (sesame seed paste), page 41
60 ml (4 tbsp) water
90 ml (6 tbsp) fresh lemon juice
Salt and freshly ground black pepper, to taste
Chopped fresh parsley, (garnish)
Sesame Pitas, page 22, cut into wedges

1. Place the cauliflower, broccoli, and yellow and red peppers in a medium salad bowl.

2. Whisk together the garlic, tahini, water, lemon juice, salt, and pepper in a small bowl.

3. Pour the dressing over the salad and toss gently to coat. Taste to correct seasonings. Refrigerate, covered, to chill. Serve on a platter. Garnish with the chopped parsley and surround with pita wedges.

Makes 6 servings.

Boxing Day Lunch

Turkey Salad Sesame in Wholemeal Honey Pitas topped with Cranberry Sauce
Carrot, Orange, and Radish Salad
Cauliflower and Onion Pickles
Pita Apple Crisps
Spiced Aniseed Tea

FETA CHEESE AND CUCUMBER SALAD

This easy-to-assemble salad is simply an arrangement of chopped cucumber and onion on a serving platter, topped with a blend of feta cheese, olive oil, yogurt, and lemon juice. It makes a marvellous accompaniment to *Kibbeh* (Middle Eastern Meatballs), page 51.

1 medium cucumber, peeled and chopped
1 small red onion, chopped
75 g (3 oz) crumbled feta cheese
30 ml (2 tbsp) olive oil
30 ml (2 tbsp) yogurt, preferably homemade, page 32
15 ml (1 tbsp) fresh lemon juice
Salt and freshly ground black pepper, to taste
Fresh mint, finely chopped, or crumbled dried mint (garnish)
Chopped spring onions (garnish)
Poppy-Seed Pita Crisps, page 28

1. Arrange the cucumber and onion on a medium platter.

2. Place the feta cheese in a small bowl. Add the oil, yogurt, lemon juice, salt, and pepper. Mix thoroughly. Taste to correct seasonings.

3. Pour the dressing over the cucumber and onion. Garnish with the mint and onions. Refrigerate, covered, to chill. Serve with poppy-seed pita crisps on the side.

Makes 4 servings.

CUCUMBER AND YOGURT SALAD

A classic Middle Eastern salad—you can put this together in moments.

450 ml (¾ pint) yogurt, preferably homemade, page 32
1 small clove garlic, crushed
2 medium cucumbers, peeled and sliced
15 ml (1 tbsp) chopped fresh mint
Salt and freshly ground black pepper, to taste
Herbed Zahter Pitas, page 26, cut into wedges

Combine all the ingredients except for the pita in a medium bowl and stir gently to blend. Taste to correct seasonings. Refrigerate, covered, to chill. Serve with zahter pita wedges.

Makes about 800 g (1¾ lb).

CARROT, ORANGE, AND RADISH SALAD

This spicy Moroccan salad, often served alongside couscous, is also a tempting topping for a chicken- or seafood-filled pita. The combination of orange and lemon juice adds a new twist to a basic dressing.

450 g (1 lb) carrots, peeled and grated
1 large orange, peeled, segmented, and cut into bite-sized chunks
75 g (3 oz) thinly sliced radishes
15 g (½ oz) finely chopped fresh coriander
45 ml (3 tbsp) olive oil
30 ml (2 tbsp) fresh lemon juice
30 ml (2 tbsp) fresh orange juice
Dash of orange-blossom water
Pinch of ground cinnamon
Salt and freshly ground black pepper, to taste
Wholemeal Honey Pitas, page 23, cut into wedges

1. Combine the carrots, orange, radishes, and coriander in a medium salad bowl.

2. Whisk together the olive oil, lemon juice, orange juice, orange-blossom water, cinnamon, salt, and pepper in a small bowl.

3. Pour the dressing over the salad and toss gently to coat. Taste to correct seasonings. Refrigerate, covered, to chill. Serve on a platter surrounded by pita wedges.

Makes 6 servings.

CLASSIC MEDITERRANEAN SALAD
(Salata)

Called *Salata,* meaning salad, this lovely toss of crisp lettuce, tomatoes, cucumbers, green

1 medium head Cos lettuce, leaves torn into bite-sized pieces
3 small tomatoes, cut into wedges
1 medium cucumber, sliced
1 small green pepper, cored, seeded, and thinly sliced

1 small onion, cut into rings
6 radishes, thinly sliced
15 g (½ oz) chopped fresh parsley
75 ml (3 fl oz) olive oil
45 ml (3 tbsp) fresh lemon juice or more, to taste

pepper, onion, radishes, and parsley is traditionally served with almost every meal in the Middle East. Its piquant personality stems from a simple dressing of olive oil, lemon juice, and just the right amount of salt and pepper.

1 clove garlic, crushed
Salt and freshly ground black
    pepper, to taste
5 ml (1 tsp) crumbled dried mint
Poppy-seed Pitas page 22, cut into
    halves

1.   Combine the lettuce, tomatoes, cucumber, green pepper, onion, radishes, and parsley in a large salad bowl.

2.   Whisk together the olive oil, lemon juice, garlic, salt, pepper, and mint in a small bowl.

3.   Pour the dressing over the salad and toss gently to coat. Taste to correct seasonings. Serve immediately with warm pita halves.

Makes 6 to 8 servings.

Variation *Chopped Vegetable Salad:* To serve as a topping for a pita sandwich or as an appetizer relish, omit the lettuce and chop all the vegetables into 1 cm (½ inch) dice. Toss with just enough dressing to season to taste.

TOMATO AND ONION SALAD

The classic Middle Eastern Tomato Salad is made with sliced onion tossed gently with tomatoes and laced with a hefty serving of olive oil, lemon juice, and mint. Here, I've also added spring onions, garlic, and coriander. It is tasty alongside meat entrées, and is a piquant topping for Falafel, page 107.

6 medium tomatoes, cut into small
    wedges
4 spring onions, chopped
1 small red onion, thinly sliced
30 ml (2 tbsp) finely chopped fresh
    coriander
15 ml (1 tbsp) finely chopped fresh
    mint or 5 ml (1 tsp) crumbled
    dried mint
60 ml (4 tbsp) olive oil
45 ml (3 tbsp) fresh lemon juice
1 clove garlic, crushed
Salt and freshly ground black
    pepper, to taste
Poppy-seed Pitas, page 22, cut into
    wedges

1.   Combine the tomatoes, spring onions, onion, coriander, and mint in a salad bowl.

2.   Whisk together the oil, lemon juice, garlic, salt, and pepper in a small bowl.

3.   Pour the dressing over the tomato mixture and toss gently to coat. Taste to correct seasonings. Refrigerate, covered, to chill. Serve with poppy-seed pita wedges.

Makes 6 to 8 servings.

CURRIED SPINACH, WALNUT, AND ORANGE SALAD

Crisp spinach leaves with crunchy walnuts and chunks of sweet orange fairly shimmer with a lacing of a curry-spiced dressing spiked with a dash of Ginger-Sultana Chutney. Serve this flavourful salad alongside a curry-filled pita pocket.

75 g (3 oz) sultanas
275 g (10 oz) fresh spinach, rinsed, and patted dry, stems trimmed, and leaves torn into bite-sized pieces
3 spring onions, chopped
1 large orange, peeled and diced
50 g (2 oz) chopped walnuts
75 ml (¾ pint) olive oil
45 ml (3 tbsp) white wine vinegar
5 ml (1 tsp) sugar
2.5 ml (½ tsp) ground cumin
2.5 ml (½ tsp) Madras curry powder
Ginger-Sultana Chutney, to taste, page 137
Salt and freshly ground black pepper, to taste
Wholemeal Honey Pitas, page 23, cut into halves

1. Soak the sultanas in boiling water until they are plumped, about 5 to 10 minutes. Drain thoroughly and dry with kitchen paper.

2. Combine the spinach, onions, orange, walnuts, and sultanas in a large salad bowl.

3. Whisk together the olive oil, vinegar, sugar, cumin, curry powder, chutney, salt and pepper.

4. Pour the dressing over the salad and toss gently to coat. Taste to correct seasonings. Serve immediately and surround with freshly made wholemeal honey pita halves.

Makes 6 servings.

Autumn Patio Supper

Oriental Prawn and Black Bean Dip with Wholemeal Honey Pita wedges
Orange-Gingered Chicken in Poppy-Seed Pitas
Curried Spinach, Walnut and Orange Salad
Pistachio and Banana Toffee Rolls with Grand Marnier Syrup and Crème Fraîche
Mint Tea

MINTED POTATO SALAD

This chunky potato salad, rich in olive oil and lemon juice and the assertive flavour of mint, is a favourite accompaniment to the myriad lamb dishes of the Middle East. It goes particularly well with classic Shish Kebabs, page 112, especially for an outdoor barbecue. Make it several hours before serving as it tastes even better if it has had a chance to marinate a little. The Cabbage Salad variation is a sure-fire success when served as a topping for a Kefta Kebab in a pita, page 109.

1 kg (2½ lb) diced, boiled small
*   potatoes*
4 spring onions, finely chopped
105 ml (7 tbsp) finely chopped fresh
*   parsley*
100 ml (4 fl oz) olive oil
75 ml (3 fl oz) fresh lemon juice
15 ml (1 tbsp) chopped fresh mint or
*   5 ml (1 tsp) crumbled dried mint*
Salt and freshly ground black
*   pepper, to taste*
Griddle-Baked Pitas, page 31

1. Combine the potatoes, spring onions, and parsley in a large salad bowl.

2. Whisk together the olive oil, lemon juice, mint, salt, and pepper in a small bowl.

3. Pour the dressing over the salad and toss gently to coat. Taste to correct seasonings. Refrigerate, covered, to chill. When serving, offer griddle-baked pitas alongside.

Makes 6 servings.

Variation *Minted Cabbage Salad:* Substitute 700 g (1½ lb) shredded cabbage and 1 medium clove crushed garlic for the potatoes and onions. Blend the crushed garlic with the olive oil, lemon juice, mint, salt, and pepper.

TABBOULEH

Tabbouleh, the famous bulgur salad of the Middle East, used variously as an appetizer, a topping for a pita sandwich, or as a dinner salad, has taken this country by storm. Now found in almost every deli section of supermarkets and gourmet food shops, this refreshing combination of bulgur, parsley, spring onions, tomatoes, olive oil, and lemon juice is also simple to make at home. What follows is a classic recipe for you to use as a general guideline, but vary it to suit your personal taste! Many people like to add crushed garlic for added zest.

175 g (6 oz) bulgur
3 medium tomatoes, chopped
4 spring onions, chopped
75 g (3 oz) finely chopped fresh parsley
15 g (½ oz) finely chopped fresh mint
225 ml (8 fl oz) olive oil
50–75 ml (2–3 fl oz) fresh lemon juice, to taste
Salt and freshly ground black pepper, to taste
Cos lettuce leaves
Wholemeal Honey Pitas, page 23, cut into halves

1.   Rinse the bulgur and place it in a medium bowl. Cover with cool water and let soak until it is tender to the bite, 20 to 30 minutes. Drain thoroughly and squeeze out any excess water. Fluff to separate the grains.

2.   Combine the tomatoes, onions, parsley, and mint in a large salad bowl. Add the bulgur and toss gently.

3.   Whisk together the olive oil, lemon juice, salt, and pepper in a small bowl.

4.   Pour the dressing over the bulgur mixture and toss gently to coat. Taste to correct seasonings. Refrigerate, covered, to chill.

5.   Line a salad bowl with lettuce leaves and arrange the tabbouleh on top. Offer wholemeal honey pita halves on the side.

Makes 6 to 8 servings.

Tip

Try blending a sprinkling of cinnamon into the tabbouleh or pass cinnamon when serving.

BULGUR, FRUIT, AND CHEESE SALAD

This unusual meld of textures and flavours completely transforms the classic *tabbouleh*. Here crispy apples and Cos lettuce complement dates and cheese all nestled in tender bulgur grains and bathed in a honey-yogurt dressing. A complete meal when accompanied by warm pita, this salad without the cheese also makes a delightful accompaniment for chicken or seafood in a pita.

175 g (6 oz) bulgur
2 large firm Red eating apples, cored and diced
75 g (3 oz) chopped dates
4 springs onions, chopped
1 medium head shredded Cos lettuce
15 g (½ oz) chopped fresh coriander
15 g (½ oz) chopped fresh parsley
90 ml (6 tbsp) olive oil
60 ml (4 tbsp) fresh lemon juice
45 ml (3 tbsp) yogurt, preferably homemade, page 32
15 ml (1 tbsp) honey
2.5 ml (½ tsp) ground nutmeg
Salt and freshly ground black pepper, to taste
100g (4 oz) cubed munster cheese
75 g (3 oz) toasted slivered almonds
Wheat-Germ Honey Pitas, page 24, cut into halves

1.   Rinse the bulgur and place it in a medium bowl. Cover with cool water and let soak until it is tender to the bite, 20 to 30 minutes. Drain thoroughly and squeeze out any excess water. Fluff to separate the grains.

2.   Combine the apples, dates, spring onions, lettuce, coriander and parsley in a large salad bowl. Add the bulgur and toss gently.

3.   Whisk together the olive oil, lemon juice, yogurt, honey, nutmeg, salt, and pepper in a small bowl.

4.   Pour the dressing over the bulgur mixture and toss gently to coat. Refrigerate, covered, to chill.

5.   Just before serving, add the cheese and toasted almonds. Toss to combine and taste to correct seasonings. Serve with warm wheat-germ honey pita halves.

Makes 8 servings.

SPICY BULGUR SALAD

A first cousin to *Tabbouleh,* this bulgur salad is spiced with fresh coriander, hot radishes, and pungent fennel. Dress it all up with olive oil and lemon laced with cinnamon, cumin, and peppery cayenne and try serving it with little Coriander and Lamb Sausage patties, page 113, or Kefta Kebabs, page 109.

175 g (6 oz) bulgur
3 medium tomatoes, chopped
50 g (2 oz) fennel, cut into julienne
    strips
25 g (1 oz) chopped fresh parsley
30 ml (2 tbsp) finely chopped fresh
    coriander
4 sliced radishes
1 small head of Cos lettuce, leaves
    torn into bite-sized pieces
4 spring onions, chopped
100 ml (4 fl oz) olive oil
50–75 ml (2–3 fl oz) fresh lemon juice
1 clove garlic, crushed
5 ml (1 tsp) ground cumin
2.5 ml (½ tsp) ground cinnamon
Pinch of cayenne, or to taste
Salt and freshly ground black
    pepper, to taste
Basic Pitas, page 21, cut into halves

1. Rinse the bulgur and place it in a medium bowl. Cover with cool water and let soak until it is tender to the bite, 20 to 30 minutes. Drain thoroughly and squeeze out any excess water. Fluff to separate the grains.

2. Combine the tomatoes, fennel, parsley, coriander, radishes, lettuce, and onions in a large salad bowl. Add the bulgur and toss gently.

3. Whisk together the olive oil, lemon juice, garlic, cumin, cinnamon, cayenne, salt, and pepper in a small bowl.

4. Pour the dressing over the bulgur mixture and toss gently to coat. Taste to correct seasonings. Refrigerate, covered, to chill. Serve surrounded by warm pita halves.

Makes 6 servings.

ABOUT HERBS

When substituting dried herbs for fresh, use about ⅓ the amount; for example, 15 ml (1 tbsp) of fresh chopped basil is equivalent to 5 ml (1 tsp) dried. Crumble dried herbs with your fingers to release their flavour.

PITA BREAD SALAD
(Fattoush)

Running a close second in popularity to *Tabbouleh,* in Middle Eastern homes is Pita Bread Salad or *Fattoush,* which translates as "dampened or moist bread." I've given this version a Greek personality by adding some feta cheese and black Greek olives. Laced with a minted olive oil and lemon dressing and a sprinkling of *Zahter. Fattoush* is similar in character to a Caesar salad with the addition of crisp-toasted garlicky pita pieces. Add them last, of course, to preserve their crunchiness, and serve this salad alongside any meat, fish, or chicken-filled pita sandwich.

50 g (2 oz) butter, softened
2 cloves garlic, crushed
2 small Basic Pitas or 1 large,
    page 21
1 head of Cos lettuce, leaves torn
    into bite-sized pieces
1 medium cucumber, peeled, sliced
6 spring onions, chopped
2 medium tomatoes, cut into wedges
12 black Greek olives, pitted
150 g (5 oz) crumbled feta cheese
15 g (½ oz) chopped fresh parsley
75 ml (3 fl oz) olive oil, or more to
    taste
50 ml (2 fl oz) fresh lemon juice, or
    more to taste
30 ml (2 tbsp) chopped fresh mint
2.5 ml (½ tsp) zahter, page 166
Salt and freshly ground black pepper
    to taste

1.   Preheat the grill.

2.   In a small bowl, cream the butter with 1 of the cloves of crushed garlic until blended.

3.   Split the pitas into rounds and spread the insides with the garlic butter. Place on the grill rack and toast until lightly browned, and well dried out. Break into bite-sized pieces.

4.   Combine the lettuce, cucumber, onions, tomatoes, olives, feta, and parsley in a large salad bowl.

5.   Whisk together the olive oil, lemon juice, remaining clove of crushed garlic, mint, zahter, salt, and pepper in a small bowl.

6.   Pour the dressing over the salad and toss gently to coat. Add the toasted pita pieces and toss again. Taste to correct seasonings and serve immediately.

Makes 6 servings.

MARKET SALAD WITH BASILICA VINAIGRETTE

This market basket full of fresh green vegetables marinated in pesto vinaigrette and tossed with diced basilica and slivers of prosciutto is irresistible with freshly baked **Wholemeal Honey Pitas.**

2 medium carrots, peeled and cut into bite-sized pieces
1 medium courgette, cut into bite-sized pieces
2 sticks celery, cut into bite-sized pieces
Two 200 g (7 oz) cans artichoke hearts, drained
Small radishes, cut in half
100 g (4 oz) mange tout, tips and strings removed
6 mushrooms, halved
50 g (2 oz) chopped spring onions
100 g (4 oz) cherry tomatoes, halved
175 ml (6 fl oz) olive oil
1 small clove garlic, crushed
45 ml (3 tbsp) fresh lemon juice
45 ml (3 tbsp) wine vinegar
15 ml (1 tbsp) chopped fresh basil or 5 ml (1 tsp) crumbled dried basil
2.5 ml (½ tsp) dry mustard, optional
Salt and freshly ground black pepper, to taste
225 g (8 oz) diced basilica
8 thin slices prosciutto, slivered
Lettuce leaves
Fresh basil leaves (garnish)
Black Greek olives, pitted (garnish)
Wholemeal Honey Pitas, page 23, cut into halves

1. Cook the carrots, courgette, and celery in boiling salted water until crisp-tender, about 3 to 5 minutes. Drain and rinse under cold running water; drain well.

2. Combine the cooked vegetables with the artichoke hearts, radishes, mange tout, mushrooms, onions, and tomatoes in a large salad bowl.

3. Whisk together the olive oil, garlic, lemon juice, vinegar, basil, mustard, salt, and pepper in a medium bowl.

4. Pour the dressing over the vegetables and toss gently to coat. Cover and marinate in the refrigerator for at least 1 hour.

5. Before serving, add the basilica and prosciutto and toss. Taste to correct seasonings. Drain any excess dressing.

6. Serve in chilled individual glass bowls lined with lettuce leaves. Sprinkle with basil leaves and olives. Pass baskets of warm pita.

Makes 8 servings.

Note: Basilica is an appetizing cheese layered with basil and pine nuts. It is available in most cheese shops and in finer supermarkets.

CHEF'S COUSCOUS SALAD

To North Africans there is only one way to do *couscous*—steamed in a *couscousière* and served with a variety of vegetables, lamb, and chicken, then accompanied by a choice of sweet and tart salads and a good peppery hot sauce. Well, I won't disagree. But how about combining some cool crisp greens with fruit, vegetables, cold meats, and bulgur and coating them lightly with a zesty orange poppy-seed dressing. *Couscous?* Not quite, but surely a close cousin.

*1 medium Cos lettuce, leaves
    separated and torn into bite-sized
    pieces*
175 g (6 oz) bulgur
100 g (4 oz) sultanas
*175 g (6 oz) cooked chickpeas,
    page 40*
100 g (4 oz) sliced radishes
*350 g (12 oz) julienned lean roasted
    lamb*
*1 whole cooked chicken breast,
    skinned, boned, and cut into
    julienne strips*
*1 orange, peeled, segmented, and cut
    into bite-sized chunks*
*225 g (8 oz) mozzarella cheese,
    grated*
30 ml (2 tbsp) fresh orange juice
30 ml (2 tbsp) fresh lemon juice
75 ml (3 fl oz) olive oil
30 ml (2 tbsp) honey
15 ml (1 tbsp) poppy seeds
*Salt and freshly ground black
    pepper, to taste*
*Wheat-Germ Honey Pitas, page 24,
    cut into wedges*
Ginger-Sultana Chutney, page 137

1. Wrap the lettuce in kitchen paper and refrigerate to chill.

2. Rinse the bulgur and place it in a medium bowl. Cover with cool water and let soak until it is tender to the bite, 20 to 30 minutes. Drain thoroughly and squeeze out any excess water. Fluff to separate the grains.

3. Meanwhile, soak the sultanas in boiling water until they are plumped, about 5 to 10 minutes. Drain thoroughly and dry with kitchen paper.

4. Combine the lettuce, bulgur, sultanas, chickpeas, radishes, lamb, chicken, orange, and cheese in a large salad bowl.

5. Whisk together the orange juice, lemon juice, olive oil, honey, poppy seeds, salt, and pepper.

6. Pour the dressing over the salad and toss gently to coat. Taste to correct seasonings. Refrigerate, covered, to chill.

7. Serve with warm wheat-germ honey pita wedges. Offer ginger-sultana chutney alongside for guests to add as they please.

Makes 8 servings.

PITA INSIDES

n America, pitas are most often stuffed to become a meal rolled up into one neat little menu-in-a-pocket.

The choices of what you can put in a pita are limitless. I've included a sampling of Middle Eastern classics such as *Shish Kebab* and *Falafel*, plus a variety of super salad sandwiches. In addition, there are loads of quick hot and cold deli sandwich ideas to get your creative juices flowing.

ut that's not all. I've also created some wonderful curries for use especially with pitas—the sauces are thicker so they won't drip through the bread. To round off this section I have some eclectic dishes—from Pita Burritos to Gingered Tofu and Vegetable Toss—that draw from just about every ethnic heritage, and highlight just how versatile pita can be.

CLASSIC PARSLEY AND ONION OMELETTE
(Aijee)

This popular Mediterranean omelette is called *Aijee*. It can be prepared as a single, large, thick omelette similar to a frittata and cut into wedges for a cocktail appetizer or made into several small omelettes to be served inside pitas.

8 eggs
15 ml (1 tbsp) fresh lemon juice
30 ml (2 tbsp) chopped fresh parsley
50 g (2 oz) chopped spring onions
15 ml (1 tbsp) chopped fresh mint
Salt and freshly ground black
　　pepper, to taste
40 g (1½ oz) butter
Sesame Pitas, page 22, cut into
　　wedges
Snipped fresh chives (garnish)
Chopped tomato (garnish)

1.　Preheat the grill.

2.　Break the eggs into a large bowl. Add the lemon juice, and beat until light and foamy. Add the parsley, onions, mint, salt, and pepper and blend well.

3.　Melt the butter in a 25.5 cm (10 inch) frying pan. Add the egg mixture and cook over medium heat, carefully lifting the edges of the omelette to allow the uncooked eggs to run underneath, until the bottom is lightly browned, about 5 minutes. Cover, lower the heat, and continue cooking until the top is completely set, 2 to 3 minutes.

4.　Uncover the pan and place under the grill until the top is browned, 2 to 3 minutes. Remove from the grill and cut into wedges. The omelette may be served either hot or cold. Place wedges of the omelette in the pita wedges and garnish with the chives and tomatoes.

Makes 4 to 6 servings.

Omelettes are perfect fillings for medium-size pita halves. Make in a 15 cm (6 inch) omelette pan and fill them with your favourite goodies such as thinly sliced tomatoes, grated Gruyère or Cheddar cheese, chopped parsley, basil and/or spring onions. They nest snugly in the pocket for out-of-hand eating.

FALAFEL
(Chickpea Croquettes)

F*alafel*, enticing herbed croquettes popular as pushcart food all over the world, are as old as Middle Eastern cuisine itself. In Israel they are made with chickpeas or a combination of broad beans and chickpeas while in Egypt they are primarily made with broad beans and called *Taamiya*. If you like it hot, add a touch of Harissa.

250 g (9 oz) dried chickpeas, cooked and drained (see page 40)
1 onion, chopped
45 ml (3 tbsp) chopped fresh parsley
3 cloves garlic, crushed
1 egg
2.5 ml (½ tsp) bicarbonate of soda
5 ml (1 tsp) ground coriander
5 ml (1 tsp) ground cumin
Salt and freshly ground black pepper, to taste
15–30 ml (1–2 tbsp) plain white flour plus additional flour for coating patties
Vegetable oil, for frying
Small Basic Pitas, page 21, with the tops off
Chopped Vegetable Salad, page 95
Dash of Harissa (Hot Pepper Sauce), optional (recipe follows)

1.   Place the chickpeas in a blender or food processor fitted with the metal blade. Add the onion, parsley, garlic, egg, bicarbonate of soda, spices, salt, pepper, and flour, process until smooth. Place in a glass bowl and refrigerate, covered, until firm, about 20 to 30 minutes.

2.   Shape into 10 to 12 patties. Dust lightly on all sides with flour.

3.   Pour the oil to a depth of 1 cm (½ inch) in a frying pan and heat until hot but not smoking. Working in batches, fry the patties turning frequently until browned and crisp, about 2 to 3 minutes. Drain on kitchen paper.

4.   Put a croquette in each pita pocket. Top with chopped vegetable salad, and a little *harissa*. To store any remaining croquettes, refrigerate, covered, for up to 1 week.

Makes 10 to 12 patties.

Variations *Taratour Falafel:* Substitute shredded lettuce, chopped tomato, and spring onions for the chopped vegetable salad and lace with Taratour, (sesame and garlic sauce), page 65.

Egyptian Bean Croquettes (Taamiya): Substitute broad beans for the chickpeas in step 1. Broad beans impart more of a vegetable flavour than the nuttier chickpeas.

HARISSA
(Hot Pepper Sauce)

This hot pepper sauce, a native of North Africa, is often used to accompany couscous. Use a little as a dressing for pita sandwiches or as a dip with pita crisps.

225 g (8 oz) hot red chillies,
　　stemmed, seeded, and chopped
6 cloves garlic, peeled
5 ml (1 tsp) caraway seeds
5 ml (1 tsp) salt
7.5 ml (1½ tsp) freshly ground black
　　pepper
7.5 ml (1½ tsp) ground cumin
5 ml (1 tsp) ground coriander
Olive oil

1. Place the chillies and garlic in a blender or food processor fitted with the metal blade. Process until coarsely ground.

2. Add the remaining ingredients except the olive oil and process until almost smooth. To store, place in a small jar, top with a thin layer of olive oil, and refrigerate until ready to use.

Makes about 225 ml (8 fl oz).

Variation Add chopped roasted pepper or diced tomato to *Harissa* for variety.

KEFTA KEBABS

Kefta is a finely minced meat mixture much like American hamburger but spiced with onion and parsley. It is shaped into sausage-like burgers on a skewer and grilled to a succulent turn. These are traditionally made in the Middle East with minced lamb, although beef seasoned in the same manner is equally good. I prefer lamb and find it easy to mince along with the other ingredients in a food processor. Use either the leg or shoulder. Cut out most of the fat and gristle, but leave a little fat to enhance the flavour.

450 g (1 lb) lean minced lamb or beef
1 small onion, minced
45 ml (3 tbsp) chopped fresh parsley
1.25 ml (¼ tsp) ground cinnamon
Pinch of allspice
Salt and freshly ground black pepper, to taste
4 small Sesame Pitas, page 22, with the tops cut off
Shredded iceberg lettuce (garnish)
Chopped tomato (garnish)
Thinly sliced red onion (garnish)
Yogurt-Garlic Sauce, page 52

1. Combine the lamb, onion, parsley, cinnamon, allspice, salt, and pepper in a large bowl; blend well. Refrigerate, covered, to chill until firm.

2. Prepare a bowl of ice and water. Divide the mixture into 4 balls. Insert a metal skewer into the centre of each ball. Dipping your hands into the bowl of ice and water to prevent the meat from sticking to them, mould each ball into a sausage shape around the skewer. Taper each end to secure the kebabs on to the skewers. (If desired, omit the skewers and mould the meat into rounded oval or flat patties.)

3. Preheat the grill.

4. Place the skewers or patties on a grill pan, about 5–7.5 cm (2–3 inches) from the heat. Grill, turning frequently, 5 to 6 minutes for rare, 7 to 8 minutes for medium, and 10 minutes for well done.

5. To serve, put a kefta kebab in each pita pocket. Garnish with the shredded lettuce, chopped tomato, and sliced onion, and lace with Yogurt-Garlic Sauce.

Makes 4 kefta kebab sandwiches.

Note: To grill the kebabs over barbecue coals, first prepare the coals. Grill about 7.5–10 cm (3–4 inches) above the coals, turning frequently, 5 to 6 minutes for rare, 7 to 8 minutes for medium, and 10 minutes for well done.

Variation *Appetizer Meatball Kebabs:* Divide the meat mixture into smaller balls. Arrange on skewers or pan fry, turning frequently, until evenly browned, about 10 minutes. Serve with *Taratour* (sesame and garlic sauce), page 65, and surround with fresh pita wedges.

Makes about 10 to 20 balls, depending on size.

GARLICKY SEAFOOD KEBABS

Mediterranean fishermen and cooks marinate these prawns and scallops in super-garlicked olive oil and lemon juice seasoned with a pinch of salt and a twist or two of freshly ground black pepper. These seafood and broccoli *kebabs* topped with *Taratour* and wrapped in a pita are simply luscious.

700 g (1½ lb) (about 18) large prawns shelled and deveined
700 g (1½ lb) (about 18) scallops rinsed and drained
100 ml (4 fl oz) olive oil
50 ml (2 fl oz) fresh lemon juice
2 cloves garlic, crushed
Salt and freshly ground black pepper, to taste
12 broccoli florets, parboiled
Taratour (sesame and garlic sauce), page 65
Griddle-Baked Pitas, page 31

1.   Place the prawns and scallops in a large shallow glass dish. Combine the oil, lemon juice, garlic, salt, and pepper in a small bowl. Blend well and pour over the seafood. Cover and marinate in the refrigerator, turning the pieces occasionally, for about 2 hours.

2.   Preheat the grill.

3.   Remove the seafood from the marinade, reserving the marinade. Thread the prawns, scallops, and broccoli florets evenly on 6 skewers.

4.   Place the skewers on a grill pan about 18–20.5 cm (7–8 inches) from the heat. Grill, turning frequently and basting with the reserved marinade, until the seafood is opaque, about 8 to 10 minutes.

5.   Wrap a griddle-baked pita around each kebab and remove the skewer. Serve laced with Taratour.

Note: To grill the kebabs over barbecue coals, first prepare the coals. Thread the seafood and broccoli on skewers and grill 7.5–10 cm (3–4 inches) above the coals, turning frequently and basting with the reserved marinade, until the seafood is opaque, about 8 to 10 minutes.

Makes 6 servings.

THE FAMOUS YOGURT DRINK

All over the Middle East, in the Balkan countries, and in India, yogurt is widely acclaimed as a health-giving food and drink.

YOGURT PINEAPPLE COOLER

This almost, but not quite, sweet yogurt drink is especially good with a chicken, egg, or seafood salad-in-a-pita!

450 ml (¾ pint) yogurt, preferably homemade, page 32
450 ml (¾ pint) unsweetened pineapple juice
100 g (4 oz) drained crushed pineapple
Mint sprigs (garnish)

Place the yogurt in a blender. Add the pineapple juice and crushed pineapple. Blend until smooth. Refrigerate, covered, to chill for at least 1 hour. Stir the yogurt mixture thoroughly just before serving and pour it into chilled tumblers. Garnish with the mint sprigs.

Variation *Fresh Fruit Shakes:* Substitute water or apple juice for the pineapple juice and add your favourite fresh fruits such as raspberries, peaches, strawberries, oranges, or bananas. Sweeten with honey or a pinch of sugar, if desired.

SAVOURY YOGURT AND MINT SHAKE WITH GARLIC

This zesty combination of yogurt and garlic, lightly seasoned with fresh mint is a lovely minty green cooler that is super served with a Garlicky Seafood Kebab in a Griddle-Baked Pita wrap.

450 ml (¾ pint) yogurt, preferably homemade, page 32
450 ml (¾ pint) iced water
1 clove garlic, cut in half
Salt, to taste
6 mint sprigs
Freshly ground black pepper (garnish)

Place the yogurt, water, garlic, salt, and 2 mint sprigs in a blender. Blend until smooth. Taste to correct seasonings. Refrigerate, covered, to chill for at least 1 hour. Stir the yogurt mixture thoroughly just before serving and pour it into chilled tumblers. Garnish with the remaining mint sprigs and a few twists of pepper.

Both fruit and savoury yogurt shakes make 4 servings.

SHISH KEBABS

Shish Kebab simply means meat grilled on a skewer and it is traditionally cooked in this manner throughout the Middle East. At just about every street corner in New York City, there is a pushcart peddling meats grilled on bamboo skewers and served on top of pitas, usually the flat Greek versions without pockets. I've marinated the lamb cubes in white wine blended with just the right amount of lemon and olive oil to enhance their delicate flavour. *Tabbouleh* is a natural companion.

900 g (2 lb) lamb, shoulder or leg, cut into 4 cm (1½ inch) cubes
225 ml (8 fl oz) dry white wine
50 ml (2 fl oz) fresh lemon juice
100 ml (4 fl oz) olive oil
Salt and freshly ground black pepper, to taste
1 medium onion, sliced
2 cloves garlic, sliced
6 button onions, cut in half
6 cherry tomatoes
1 large green pepper, cored, seeded, and cut into 12 chunks
6 medium Poppy-Seed Pitas, page 22, with the tops cut off

1.   Place the lamb in a large, shallow dish. Combine the wine, lemon juice, oil, salt, pepper, sliced onion, and garlic in a medium bowl. Blend well and pour over the lamb. Cover and marinate in the refrigerator, turning the lamb occasionally, for several hours or overnight. (The longer the lamb marinates, the more tender it becomes.)

2.   Preheat the grill.

3.   Remove the lamb from the marinade, reserving the marinade. Thread the lamb, onion halves, cherry tomatoes, and green pepper chunks evenly on 6 skewers.

4.   Place the skewers on a grill pan about 5–7.5 cm (2–3 inches) from the heat. Grill, turning frequently and basting with the reserved marinade, 5 to 7 minutes for rare, 8 to 10 minutes for medium, and 12 to 15 minutes for well done.

5.   To serve, remove the lamb cubes and vegetables from the skewers and put them in the pita pockets while they are still warm.

Makes 6 servings.

Note: To grill the kebabs over barbecue coals, first prepare the coals, then thread the lamb on the skewers without the vegetables. Grill 10–12.5 cm (4–5 inches) above the coals, turning frequently and basting with the reserved marinade, 5 to 7 minutes for rare, 8 to 10 minutes for medium, and 12 to 15 minutes for well done.

To grill the vegetables, thread the onions and peppers on 1 skewer. Thread the tomatoes on a second skewer. Grill 10–12.5 cm (4–5 inches) above the coals, turning frequently and basting with the reserved marinade, 15 to 18 minutes for the onions and peppers, about 5 to 8 minutes for the tomatoes.

Variation *Shish Kebab in Yogurt Marinade:* Substitute Yogurt Marinade for the oil and lemon marinade above: Combine 450 ml (¾ pint) yogurt (preferably homemade, page 32), 1 or 2 crushed garlic cloves, 1 small minced onion, 5 ml (1 tsp) ground coriander, and 2.5 ml (½ tsp) crumbled dried mint in a small bowl. Blend thoroughly and pour the marinade over the lamb. Cover and refrigerate as above.

CORIANDER AND LAMB SAUSAGE PATTIES
(Mahnik)

These succulent little lamb sausages are simple to make and a treat to eat! I've added just enough fat to make them tasty and moist, although if you want a completely low-fat sausage, simply omit the fat. Slipped into a pita pocket with herb-scambled eggs, they are an excellent brunch or breakfast offering. They also make a hearty sandwich when accompanied by a Classic Mediterranean Salad, page 94.

900 g (2 lb) minced lean lamb
225 g (8 oz) minced lamb fat
  (optional)
100 ml (4 fl oz) hearty red wine
60 ml (4 tbsp) whole coriander
  seeds
5 ml (1 tsp) ground coriander
2.5 ml (½ tsp) allspice
2.5 ml (½ tsp) ground cinnamon
Salt and freshly ground black
  pepper, to taste
Vegetable oil, for frying
Griddle-Baked Pitas, page 31

1. Mix together the minced lamb and lamb fat in a large shallow dish. Combine the remaining ingredients except the pita in a small bowl. Blend well and pour over the lamb. Cover and marinate in the refrigerator, turning the pieces occasionally. for 3 hours. Remove the lamb from the marinade.

2. Shape 1 rounded tablespoon of the meat into a small patty. Lightly grease a frying pan and fry the patty over medium heat until browned on both sides. Taste the cooked patty and correct any seasonings in the uncooked meat.

3. Form the remaining meat into twelve 5 cm (2 inch) patties or small sausage-like rolls. (The patties can be made ahead to this point and frozen for up to 3 months in small freezer-proof plastic bags, separating each patty with a piece of cling film. Some wine will seep into the bag and serve as a marinade.)

4. Working in two batches, lightly grease a frying pan and fry the patties over medium heat until browned on both sides, about 8 to 10 minutes. Drain on kitchen paper.

5. Serve warm, wrapped in griddle-baked pitas.

Makes 12 patties or rolls.

HERB-GRILLED CHICKEN AND ONION ON A PITA

Throughout the Middle East, street or *souk* vendors sell savoury herbed chicken on top of zahter-seasoned pitas. While they season both the chicken and the pita with zahter, I've departed from tradition by offering grilled chicken marinated in olive oil, wine, and thyme, and served with an onion-pine nut sauté on top of Herbed Zahter Pitas. Served cold, it makes a wonderful picnic packet, wrapped individually in kitchen foil. I prefer it hot, however, when all the oils and juices combine to make the chicken superbly succulent. This is a marvelous dish for an outdoor barbecue (see note).

2 chickens (about 1.1–1.4 kg/2½–3 lb each), cut into quarters
225 ml (8 fl oz) olive oil
50 ml (2 fl oz) dry white wine
1 large clove garlic, crushed
3.75 ml (¾ tsp) crumbled dried thyme
Salt and freshly ground black pepper, to taste
4 medium onions, sliced
25 g (1 oz) pine nuts
8 Herbed Zahter Pitas, page 26

1.   Lay the chicken quarters in a large glass or pottery baking dish. Combine 175 ml (6 fl oz) of the oil, the wine, garlic, thyme, salt and pepper in a small bowl. Blend well and pour over the chicken. Cover and marinate in the refrigerator, turning the pieces occasionally, for several hours or overnight.

2.   Preheat the grill.

3.   Remove the chicken from the marinade, reserving the marinade. Grill, skinside down, 18–20.5 cm (7–8 inches) from the heat for about 30 minutes. Turn and brush with the marinade. Grill until tender, 15 to 30 minutes longer.

4.   Meanwhile, heat the remaining oil in a frying pan. Add the onions and pine nuts and sauté over medium heat until the onions are light yellow and the pine nuts are golden, about 8 to 10 minutes.

5.   Spoon some of the onion and nut mixture on the tops of the pitas. Top each with a grilled chicken quarter.

Makes 8 servings.

Note: To grill over barbecue coals, first prepare the coals. Place the chicken on the grill, skinside down, 15–18 cm (6–7 inches) above the coals. Grill until the skin is golden brown, about 10 minutes. Brush with the marinade. Turn and grill 20 to 30 minutes longer. Brush again with the marinade and turn, grilling 5 minutes longer on each side or until chicken is tender and crisp. Turn frequently to ensure a golden-brown surface without burning and charring the skin.

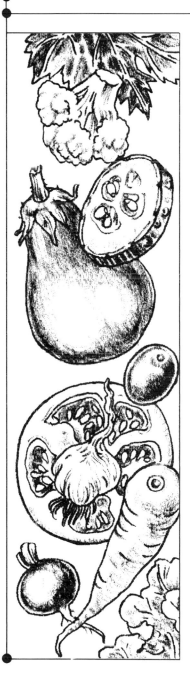

COLD PITA DELIS

Pitas make absolutely delicious deli sandwiches. Try these dandy combinations.

PITA CLUB

Spread the insides of a Basic Pita with mayonnaise and fill it with cold sliced chicken, bacon slices, thinly sliced tomato, and Cos lettuce leaves. Top it all with freshly ground black pepper.

ROAST BEEF WITH ONION

Spread a thin coating of horseradish sauce on the insides of a Sesame Pita and line it with paper-thin slices of rare roast beef, tomato, sweet pickles, and red onion.

PRAWN SALAD AND SESAME

Line a Wholemeal Honey Pita with lettuce and fill it with prawn salad, sliced artichoke hearts, and chopped spring onions. Crown it with a sprinkling of toasted sesame seeds.

CHICKEN SALAD WITH YOGURT CHEESE AND BLACK OLIVES

Spread the insides of a Wheat-Germ Honey Pita with yogurt cheese. Fill with chicken salad sprinkled with chopped almonds. Top it with chopped black Greek Olives.

LIVERWURST, SLICED EGG, AND SPRING ONIONS

Season the insides of a Basic Pita with a mustardy mayonnaise and layer thin slices of liverwurst and hard-boiled egg sprinkled with chopped spring onions. Add some crisp lettuce leaves.

TOFU, AVOCADO, AND ALFALFA SPROUTS

Spread the insides of a Wheat-Germ Honey Pita with a thyme-seasoned mayonnaise and fill it with chopped tofu and grated Gruyère cheese. Add sliced avocado and mushrooms topped with alfalfa sprouts and a dollop of the seasoned mayonnaise.

EGG SALAD WITH TARATOUR

Mound egg salad in a Sesame Pita, lace it with Taratour (sesame and garlic sauce) and sprinkle with toasted sesame seeds.

CHICKEN SALAD SESAME

There are probably as many varieties of chicken salad as there are chickens in the world, but I think this recipe is particularly tasty. The addition of Tahini and yogurt gives it a piquant nutty verve. Fill pitas with this unusual mix and garnish with toasted sesame seeds.

450 g (1 lb) cooked diced chicken
100 g (4 oz) diced celery
100 g (4 oz) seedless green grapes, cut in half
50 g (2 oz) toasted pine nuts
90 ml (6 tbsp) mayonnaise
60 ml (4 tbsp) yogurt, preferably homemade, page 32
30 ml (2 tbsp) Tahini (sesame seed paste), page 41
Salt and freshly ground black pepper, to taste
Small Sesame Pitas, page 22, with the tops cut off
Cos lettuce leaves
Toasted sesame seeds (garnish)
Additional grape halves (garnish)

1. Combine the chicken, celery, grapes, and pine nuts in a large bowl.

2. Whisk together the mayonnaise, yogurt, tahini, salt, and pepper in a small bowl.

3. Fold the dressing into the chicken salad and toss gently to coat. Taste to correct seasonings. Refrigerate, covered, to chill.

4. Line the pitas with the lettuce leaves and fill with the chicken salad. Garnish with toasted sesame seeds and additional grape halves.

Makes about 900 g (2 lb).

Spring Terrace Luncheon

White wine spritzers with kiwi and orange slices
Oriental Prawn and Black Bean Dip with Wholemeal Honey Pita wedges
Chicken Salad Sesame in Sesame Pitas
Dilled Cucumber-Salmon Salad in Wheat-Germ Honey Pitas
Pita Bread Salad
Sweet Pita Crisps with Sesame-Honey, Sesame-Carob, and Sesame-Maple Dipping Sauces
Mint Tea

CHICKEN SALAD BEARNAISE

If you like traditional Steak Béarnaise, you'll adore this Chicken Salad Béarnaise. The mixture of diced chicken, celery, spring onions, raisins, and almonds is dressed in a delicate toss of tarragon-seasoned mayonnaise, parsley, and white wine. In a pita pocket lined with iceberg lettuce leaves and topped with sliced black olives, it's scrumptious!

75 g (3 oz) raisins
450 g (1 lb) cooked diced chicken
100 g (4 oz) diced celery
2 spring onions, finely chopped
50 g (2 oz) toasted slivered almonds
100 ml (4 fl oz) mayonnaise
15 ml (1 tbsp) dry white wine
45 ml (3 tbsp) chopped parsley
5 ml (1 tsp) chopped fresh tarragon or 2.5 ml (½ tsp) crumbled dried tarragon
Salt and freshly ground black pepper, to taste
Small Wholemeal Sesame Pitas, page 24, with the tops cut off
Iceberg lettuce leaves
Sliced black Greek olives (garnish)

1. Soak the raisins in boiling water until they are plumped, about 5 to 10 minutes. Drain thoroughly and dry with kitchen paper.

2. Combine the raisins, chicken, celery, onions and almonds in a large bowl.

3. Whisk together the mayonnaise, wine, parsley, tarragon, salt, and pepper in a small bowl.

4. Fold the dressing into the chicken salad and toss gently to coat. Taste to correct seasonings. Refrigerate, covered, to chill.

5. Line the pitas with the lettuce leaves. Fill with the chicken salad and top with sliced olives.

Makes about 900 g (2 lb).

SMOKED CHICKEN AND APRICOT SALAD

The sweet and smoky blend of chicken and apricot tossed in a celery-seed mayonnaise makes a perfect filling for Wheat-Germ Honey Pitas.

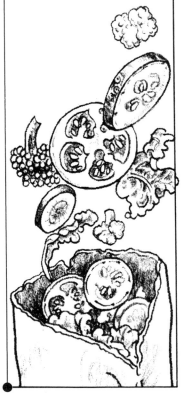

350 g (12 oz) julienned smoked chicken
100 g (4 oz) chopped celery
75 g (3 oz) finely chopped dried apricots
60 ml (4 tbsp) sweet pickle
50 g (2 oz) thinly sliced radishes
2 spring onions, chopped
100 ml (4 fl oz) mayonnaise
5 ml (1 tsp) celery seed
Salt and freshly ground black pepper, to taste
Small Wheat-Germ Honey Pitas, page 24, with the tops cut off
Shredded Cos lettuce

1. Combine the chicken, celery, apricots, pickles, radishes, and spring onions in a large bowl.

2. Whisk together the mayonnaise, celery seed, salt, and pepper in a small bowl.

3. Fold the dressing into the chicken salad and toss gently to coat. Taste to correct seasonings. Refrigerate, covered, to chill.

4. Line the pitas with the shredded lettuce and fill with the chicken salad.

Makes about 700 g (1½ lb).

Late Summer Buffet Luncheon

Herbed Bloody Marys with fresh coriander sprigs
Hummus Guacamole with Parmesan Pita Crisps
Scallop and Lemon-Ball Salad in Basic Pitas
Smoked Chicken and Apricot Salad in Wheat-Germ Honey Pitas
Cauliflower, Broccoli, and Pepper Salad
Spiced Apple Pudding with Vanilla Sauce
Iced Mint Tea

CHICKEN BROCCOLI DIVAN

I n this favourite recipe from my good friend Marian Stamos of Chicago, a touch of sherry spices up a classic chicken salad while the broccoli offers a surefire bounce in texture, colour, and vitamins.

350 g (12 oz) cooked diced chicken
225 g (8 oz) cooked chopped broccoli
75 g (1½ oz) chopped celery
100 ml (4 fl oz) mayonnaise
15 ml (1 tbsp) dry sherry
5 ml (1 tsp) Dijon mustard
2.5 ml (½ tsp) salt
2.5 ml (½ tsp) Worcestershire sauce
Small Basic Pitas, page 21, with the
   tops cut off
Shredded lettuce

1. Combine the chicken, broccoli, and celery in a large bowl.

2. Whisk together the mayonnaise, sherry, mustard, salt, and Worcestershire sauce in a small bowl.

3. Fold the dressing into the chicken salad and toss gently to coat. Taste to correct seasonings. Refrigerate, covered, to chill.

4. Line the pitas with the shredded lettuce and fill them with the chicken salad.

Makes about 450 g (1 lb).

PEANUT BUTTER AND PITA

P eanut butter is marvellous in pitas and you can vary its personality with the addition of a host of delicious ingredients. First cut medium pitas in half and spread the pockets with your favourite brand of peanut butter. Then try some of the following additions to make a special lunch box or picnic treat for children of all ages.

● Raisins and pecans or walnuts
● Apples and walnuts
● Bananas and raisins
● Crumbled bacon
● Grated carrots, raisins, and almonds
● Alfalfa sprouts, chopped dates, and macadamia nuts
● Homemade apple sauce or whole cranberry sauce
● Sliced green or red pepper

CRABMEAT, CARROT, AND GRAPE SALAD

This healthy, healthy salad tastes just as good as it is good for you!

450 g (1 lb) shelled cooked crabmeat
100 g (4 oz) diced celery
2 spring onions, finely chopped
15 ml (1 tbsp) finely chopped fresh parsley
1 carrot, peeled and grated
100 g (4 oz) seedless green grapes, cut in half
100 ml (4 fl oz) mayonnaise
50 ml (2 fl oz) yogurt, preferably homemade, page 32
5 ml (1 tsp) fresh lemon juice
5 ml (1 tsp) fresh orange juice
Salt and freshly ground black pepper, to taste
Dash of Harissa (Hot Pepper Sauce), optional, page 108
Small Wholemeal Honey Pitas, page 24, with the tops cut off
Chicory leaves

1. Combine the crabmeat, celery, onions, parsley, carrot, and grapes in a large bowl.

2. Whisk together the mayonnaise, yogurt, lemon juice, orange juice, salt, pepper, and harissa, if desired, in a small bowl.

3. Fold the dressing into the crabmeat salad and toss gently to coat. Taste to correct seasonings. Refrigerate, covered, to chill.

4. Line the pitas with the chicory and fill with the crabmeat salad.

Makes about 450 g (1 lb).

CRABMEAT AND NUT HAWAIIAN SALAD

Fruit in combination with seafood is enhanced with a light curry mayonnaise. What makes this salad especially good is a blend of macadamia nuts, pineapple, and avocado. Add a touch of papaya instead of the avocado for a change of pace!

450 g (1 lb) shelled cooked crabmeat
50 g (2 oz) diced celery
225 g (8 oz) ripe fresh pineapple chunks, cut in 1 cm (½ inch) cubes or one 227 g (8 oz) can pineapple chunks, drained and cut in 1 cm (½ inch) cubes
½ ripe avocado, pitted, peeled, and thinly sliced
100 ml (4 fl oz) mayonnaise
50 ml (2 fl oz) yogurt, preferably homemade, page 32
2.5 ml (½ tsp) Madras curry powder, or to taste
Salt and freshly ground black pepper, to taste
50 g (2 oz) coarsely chopped macadamia nuts
Small Wholemeal Honey Pitas, page 23, with the tops off
Shredded radicchio

1. Combine the crabmeat, celery, pineapple, and avocado in a large bowl.

2. Whisk together the mayonnaise, yogurt, curry powder, salt, pepper, and half of the macadamia nuts in a small bowl.

3. Fold the dressing into the crabmeat salad and toss gently to coat. Taste to correct seasonings. Refrigerate, covered, to chill.

4. Line the pitas with the shredded lettuce and fill with the crabmeat salad. Sprinkle with the remaining macadamia nuts.

Makes about 900 g (2 lb).

Lunch at the Beach

Crudités (carrot curls, celery sticks, aubergine circles) with Yogurt-Garlic Dip
Down-East Lobster Rolls in Basic Pitas
Crabmeat and Nut Hawaiian Salad in Wholemeal Honey Pitas
Pressed Apricot Rolls
Orangeade with orange-blossom water

GRILLED DELI PITAS

Fill pitas with any of the following delicious combinations. Spread the outsides with softened butter and grill them on a lightly greased frying pan or sandwich toaster until they are lightly browned and slightly crisp.

GRUYÈRE CHEESE, YELLOW PEPPER, AND HAM

Mound grated Gruyère cheese, thinly sliced tomatoes, slivers of yellow pepper, and sliced mushrooms in a Wholemeal Honey Pita. Top it with paper-thin slices of ham lightly spread with a spicy mustard.

SAUTÉED LAMB SAUSAGE AND MOZZARELLA CHEESE

Sauté crumbled Coriander and Lamb Sausage, page 113, with chopped garlic and onion. Stuff in a Sesame Pita and top with a hefty measure of Mozzarella cheese and finely chopped black Greek olives.

CUBAN CAFETERIA GRILL

Layer thinly sliced smoked ham, roast fresh pork, Gruyère cheese, and sliced dill pickles in a Basic Pita and cover it all with a light spread of prepared mustard.

MOZZARELLA CHEESE, PROSCIUTTO, AND COURGETTE

Drizzle the insides of a Poppy-Seed Pita with olive oil and a light sprinkling of chopped fresh basil, then layer thin slices of Mozzarella cheese, prosciutto, and courgette topped with chopped spring onions.

APPLE, BLUE CHEESE, AND SMOKED CHICKEN

Spread the insides of a Wheat-Germ Honey Pita with softened butter and sprinkle lightly with freshly ground black pepper. Layer thinly sliced apples and smoked chicken topped with crumbled blue cheese.

GRUYÈRE CHEESE AND MAPLE SYRUP BRUNCH SANDWICH

Mound grated Gruyère cheese inside a Sesame Pita and top with crisp bacon slices. Serve with warm pure maple syrup after removing the sandwich from the grill.

SCALLOP AND MELON-BALL SALAD

This unusual mingle of ingredients creates a pleasingly refreshing pita sandwich filling. The toasted sunflower seeds add the crowning touch.

450 g (1 lb) scallops, rinsed and
  drained
3 spring onions, finely chopped
100 ml (4 fl oz) dry white wine
2.5 ml (½ tsp) salt
15 ml (1 tbsp) fresh lime juice
50 g (2 oz) chopped celery
175 g (6 oz) diced cantalope or
  honeydew melon, cut into bite-
  sized pieces
15 ml (1 tbsp) finely chopped fresh
  coriander
100 ml (4 fl oz) mayonnaise
50 ml (2 fl oz) yogurt, preferably
  homemade, page 32
Salt and freshly ground black
  pepper, to taste
75 g (3 oz) toasted sunflower seeds
Small Basic Pitas, page 21, with the
  tops cut off
Lettuce leaves
Sliced pitted black olives (garnish)

1.   Place the scallops, ⅓ of the chopped onions, and the wine in a pan. Pour in enough water to just cover. Add the salt and bring to a boil. Reduce the heat and simmer, uncovered, until the scallops begin to change colour, about 1 minute.

Remove from the heat and let the scallops cool in the poaching liquid; drain and discard the poaching liquid. Cut them into 1 cm (½ inch) pieces.

2.   Place the scallops in a large bowl and sprinkle with the lime juice. Add the remaining onions, the celery, melon, and coriander. Toss gently to blend.

3.   Whisk together the mayonnaise, yogurt, salt, and pepper in a small bowl.

4.   Fold the dressing into the scallop salad and toss gently to coat. Refrigerate, covered, to chill.

5.   Just before serving add the sunflower seeds and toss again. Taste to correct seasonings.

6.   Line the pitas with the lettuce leaves and fill with the scallop salad. Sprinkle with the sliced black olives.

Makes about 450 g (1 lb).

CURRIED PRAWN, PERSIMMON, AND NUT SALAD

The flavourful combination of prawns, persimmon, and apple is heightened with the addition of curry powder, walnuts and poppy seeds. This makes a perfect transitional sandwich offering for the autumn and winter months when persimmons are at their sweet luscious peak. To avoid any mouth-puckering bitterness, be sure to choose ripe persimmons—they'll be a deep orange and soft.

900 g (2 lb) cooked prawns
50 g (2 oz) chopped celery
2 ripe persimmons, seeded, peeled, and chopped (they'll be slightly mashed)
1 eating apple, chopped
100 ml (4 fl oz) mayonnaise
50 ml (2 fl oz) yogurt, preferably homemade, page 32
5 ml (1 tsp) Madras curry powder
Salt and freshly ground black pepper, to taste
100 g (4 oz) chopped walnuts
40 g (1½ oz) poppy seeds
Small Wholemeal Honey Pitas, page 23, with the tops cut off
Shredded iceberg lettuce

1.   Combine the prawns, celery, persimmons, and apple in a large bowl.

2.   Whisk together the mayonnaise, yogurt, curry powder, salt, pepper, walnuts, and poppy seeds in a small bowl.

3.   Fold the dressing into the prawn salad and toss gently to coat. Taste to correct seasonings. Refrigerate, covered, to chill.

4.   Line the pitas with the shredded lettuce and fill with the prawn salad.

Makes about 1.4 kg (3 lb).

DOWN-EAST LOBSTER ROLL IN A PITA

This Down-East tradition makes a perfect filling for a pita. Blend 450 g (1 lb) freshly cooked lobster meat, cut in chunks, with 15 ml (3 tbsp) of mayonnaise and refrigerate, covered, to chill. Meanwhile, cut the tops off 4 Basic pitas, spread the insides with melted butter, wrap them in kitchen foil, and place them in a preheated 150°C (300°F) mark 2 oven until just warm, 3 to 5 minutes. Fill them with the lobster salad, sprinkle with chopped fresh parsley, and serve immediately with a tall glass of fresh lemonade! Pass lemon wedges for those seafood-with-lemon devotees!

DILLED CUCUMBER-SALMON SALAD

Cucumber and salmon are favourite teammates and here the addition of yogurt binds them closer together. The sprinkling of dill assures a perfect marriage.

2 cucumbers, peeled, halved lengthwise, seeded, and thinly sliced
Salt and freshly ground black pepper, to taste
350 g (12 oz) flaked cooked salmon, or two 213 g (7 oz) cans salmon, drained and flaked
100 ml (4 fl oz) yogurt, preferably homemade, page 32
Fresh lemon juice, to taste

50 g (2 oz) chopped celery
1 large spring onion, finely chopped
15 ml (1 tbsp) finely chopped fresh dill or 5 ml (1 tsp) dried dill
Small Wheat-Germ Honey Pitas, page 24, with the tops cut off
Lettuce leaves
Additional finely chopped fresh dill (garnish)

1. Place the cucumbers in a colander set over a medium bowl. Sprinkle lightly with salt and pepper and toss to mix. Set aside until wilted, about 15 to 20 minutes. Squeeze out the water and pat dry with kitchen paper.

2. Transfer the cucumbers into a large bowl. Add the salmon, yogurt, lemon juice, celery, onion, and dill. Toss gently to blend. Taste to correct seasonings. Refrigerate, covered, to chill.

3. Line the pitas with the lettuce leaves and fill with the cucumber-salmon salad. Garnish with the extra dill.

Makes 700 g (1½ lb).

PRICKLY PEAR, TOMATO, AND FETA SALAD

I've adapted this delightful recipe from one given to me by my good friends Edward and M'Lou Holliday in Key Biscayne, Florida. They use fresh prickly pears from the garden, cleaned, with the thorns removed, cooked briefly in boiling salted water, then refrigerated. (Before you use prickly pears, be sure to rinse and drain them thoroughly in order to remove the natural thick residue.) They serve their pricky pear salad rolled in tortillas as an appetizer, but it is equally delicious in griddle-baked pitas, topped with feta cheese and chillies. Guaranteed to arouse questions and raves!

450 g (1 lb) prickly pears peeled and sliced
2 medium tomatoes, seeded and chopped
1 small onion, finely chopped
30 ml (2 tbsp) chopped fresh coriander
45 ml (3 tbsp) olive oil
15 ml (1 tbsp) red wine vinegar
1.25 ml (¼ tsp) crumbled dried oregano
Salt and freshly ground black pepper, to taste
Griddle-Baked Pitas, page 31
Lettuce leaves
Strips of seeded fresh chillies (garnish)
Crumbled feta cheese (garnish)
Chopped fresh coriander (garnish)

1. Combine the prickly pears, tomatoes, onion, and coriander in a large bowl.

2. Whisk together the olive oil, vinegar, oregano, salt, and pepper in a small bowl.

3. Pour the dressing over the salad and toss gently to coat. Taste to correct seasonings. Refrigerate, covered, to chill.

4. Top the griddle-baked pitas with the lettuce leaves followed by the prickly pear salad. Garnish with the chilli strips. Sprinkle with feta cheese and coriander. Roll the pitas closed and serve each in squares of greaseproof paper to catch any drips.

Makes about 450 g (1 lb).

SMOKED HAM AND FRESH ASPARAGUS

This refreshing sandwich comes alive with crisp-tender fresh asparagus marinated in a piquant minted oil-and-lemon dressing. Serve it with fresh yogurt cheese and smoked ham and top it with radicchio. A perfect celebration when the first young asparagus shoots hit the market!

24 asparagus spears, cooked until crisp-tender
Freshly ground black pepper, to taste
100 ml (4 fl oz) olive oil
50 ml (2 fl oz) fresh lemon juice
5 ml (1 tsp) finely chopped fresh mint
Salt, to taste
12 thin slices of smoked ham
6 small Wheat-Germ Honey Pitas, page 24, with the tops cut off
175–225 ml (6–8 fl oz) Yogurt Cheese, page 33
Shredded radicchio

1. Trim the asparagus spears to fit inside the pitas then place the spears in a glass or pottery dish. Sprinkle with the pepper.

2. Whisk together the olive oil, lemon juice, mint, salt, and pepper in a small bowl. Pour the dressing over the asparagus. Cover and marinate in the refrigerator, turning the spears occasionally, for 2 hours.

3. Drain the asparagus, reserving the marinade. Roll 2 asparagus spears in each slice of the smoked ham. Set the rolls aside.

4. Spread the insides of the pitas with the yogurt cheese, dividing it evenly among the 6 loaves. Place two roll-ups in each pita. Top with the shredded radicchio and drizzle a little of the reserved marinade over everything.

Makes 6 sandwiches.

Summer Picnic

Herbed Hummus with Pistachios and Poppy-Seed Pita wedges
Spinach and Raisin Triangles
Smoked Ham and Fresh Asparagus in Wheat-Germ Honey Pitas
Marinated Artichokes with Peppers
Pressed Apricot Rolls
Chilled white wine
Iced Mint tea

DEVILLED EGG AND MUSHROOM SALAD

The mushrooms and shallots must be sautéed first, then laced with white wine and simmered until all the wine and water from the mushrooms has evaporated before the unique flavour of this egg salad reaches its peak.

25 g (1 oz) butter
225 g (8 oz) mushrooms, wiped clean with damp kitchen paper and chopped
30 ml (2 tbsp) chopped shallots
30 ml (2 tbsp) dry white wine
6 hard-boiled eggs, chopped
50 g (2 oz) chopped celery
100 ml (4 fl oz) mayonnaise
30 ml (2 tbsp) yogurt, preferably homemade, page 32
15 ml (1 tbsp) Dijon mustard
Salt and freshly ground black pepper, to taste
Small Basic Pitas, page 21, with the tops cut off
Alfalfa sprouts (garnish)
Snipped fresh chives (garnish)

1. Melt the butter in a frying pan. Add the mushrooms and shallots and sauté over medium heat until tender, about 5 minutes. Add the wine and cook over low heat until all the liquid has evaporated. Remove from the heat and let cool. Refrigerate, covered, to chill.

2. Place the chopped eggs in a medium bowl. Add the celery, and cooled mushrooms and shallots.

3. Whisk together the mayonnaise, yogurt, mustard, salt, and pepper in a small bowl.

4. Fold the dressing into the egg mixture and toss gently to coat. Taste to correct seasonings. Refrigerate, covered, to chill.

5. Fill the pitas with the egg salad and garnish with alfalfa sprouts and chives.

Makes about 225 g (8 oz).

OPEN-FACED PITA CHEESE MELTS

Turn a thin loaf of pita bottom side up or split thicker loaves in two, spread with softened butter, a favourite dressing, and top off with a combination of special sandwich fillings and cheese. Grill it all to a bubbly turn for a super-duper open-faced pita cheese melt.

SALMON SALAD WITH CURRIED MAYONNAISE

Spread Sesame Wholemeal Pita with curried mayonnaise and mound it with salmon salad. Top it with chopped spring onions and grated Jarlsberg cheese, sprinkled with freshly snipped dill and a squeeze of lemon juice.

REUBEN WITH DILL

Spread a Wheat-Germ Honey Pita with Dijon mustard and top it with thinly sliced, lean beef, drained sauerkraut sprinkled with caraway seeds, thinly sliced dill pickles and grated Gruyère cheese.

MIDDLE-EASTERN NACHO MELT

Spread a Sesame Pita with *Hummus Bi Tahini*. Top it with chopped fresh coriander, sliced peppers, and crumbled feta cheese, and grated Mozzarella cheese.

HAM, FONTINA, AND PINEAPPLE

Blend a little Dijon mustard with brown sugar and a pinch of ground cloves and spread it on a Wholemeal Honey Pita. Layer on thinly sliced ham, and top it with strained crushed pineapple squeezed to remove excess moisture, and sliced Fontina cheese.

CURRIED TUNA SALAD, WATERCRESS, AND CHEDDAR CHEESE

Top a Basic Pita with Curried Tuna Salad laced with chopped watercress and slivered Cheddar cheese.

MOZZARELLA, FRUIT, AND NUT SALAD

Mozzarella is marvellous tossed together with fruit in a sesame mayonnaise—a combination which makes a perfect, refreshing filling.

225 g (8 oz) seedless green grapes, cut in half
1 large green apple, cut into bite-sized pieces
225 g (8 oz) Mozzarella cheese, grated
50 ml (2 fl oz) mayonnaise
50 ml (2 fl oz) Tahini (sesame seed paste), page 41
30 ml (2 tbsp) toasted sesame seeds, page 165
15 ml (1 tbsp) fresh lemon juice
50 g (2 oz) toasted pine nuts, page 164
Small Sesame Pitas, page 22, with the tops cut off
Endive leaves

1. Combine the grapes, apple, and Mozzarella in a large bowl.

2. Whisk together the mayonnaise, tahini, toasted sesame seeds, and lemon juice in a small bowl.

3. Fold the dressing into the fruit and cheese salad and toss gently to coat. Taste to correct seasonings. Refrigerate, covered, to chill.

4. Just before serving, add 90 ml (6 tbsp) of the pine nuts and toss again. Line the pitas with the endive leaves and fill with the fruit and cheese salad. Sprinkle with the remaining toasted pine nuts.

Makes about 700 g (1½ lb).

Variations In place of the grapes and apple, substitute equal amounts of any of the following fruits or use a combination of several of them: pineapples, pears, fresh or dried figs, papayas, mangoes, and peaches.

SESAME-TOSSED PEAR WALDORF AND CHEESE

The Waldorf Astoria Hotel in New York, where the apple version of the Waldorf salad originated, might not recognize this one, but it surely is a winner! The subtle flavour of pear fairly screams for the piquant blue-cheese crumbles and the distinctive flavour of the ginger. And the Tahini-honey dressing melds everything together into a scrumptious salad.

75 g (3 oz) raisins
4 peeled and diced pears
100 g (4 oz) chopped celery
50 g (2 oz) chopped walnuts or
*   pecans*
2.5 ml (½ tsp) ground ginger
50 ml (2 fl oz) mayonnaise
50 ml (2 fl oz) Tahini, (sesame seed
*   paste), page 41*
30 ml (2 tbsp) toasted sesame seeds,
*   page 165*
15 ml (1 tbsp) fresh lemon juice
5 ml (1 tsp) honey
50 g (2 oz) crumbled blue cheese, or
*   more to taste*
Small Wholemeal Sesame Pitas,
*   page 24, with the tops cut off*
Whole walnuts or pecans (garnish)

1. Soak the raisins in boiling water until they are plumped, about 5 to 10 minutes. Drain thoroughly and dry with kitchen paper.

2. Combine the pears, celery, nuts, raisins, and ginger in a large bowl.

3. Whisk together the mayonnaise, tahini, sesame seeds, lemon juice, and honey in a small bowl.

4. Fold the dressing into the fruit salad and toss gently to coat. Sprinkle with the blue cheese and toss again to mix. Taste to correct seasonings. Refrigerate, covered, to chill.

5. Spoon the salad into the pitas. Garnish with whole walnuts or pecans.

Makes about 700 g (1½ lb).

CARROT AND BANANA CURRY

(With Cashew-Sultana Chutney)

This enticingly simple vegetable-fruit curry is perfect for a pita pocket. It is essentially a carrot and banana toss, seasoned with the traditional spices so characteristically associated with this Indian dish. The yogurt imparts an important tanginess and a creamy light coating to carry the flavours of the spices.

50 ml (2 fl oz) vegetable oil
2.5 ml (½ tsp) turmeric
2.5 ml (½ tsp) ground cumin
15 ml (1 tbsp) peeled and slivered fresh ginger
2.5 ml (½ tsp) ground cardamom
1.25 ml (¼ tsp) caraway seeds
350 g (12 oz) ripe, firm bananas, cut in 1 cm (½ inch) pieces
350 g (12 oz) carrots, peeled and cut in 0.5 cm (¼ inch) diagonal slices
Salt, to taste
Crushed dried chilli flakes, to taste
5 ml (1 tsp) Madras curry powder
100 ml (4 fl oz) fresh orange juice
Dash of fresh lemon juice, or to taste
225 ml (8 fl oz) yogurt, preferably homemade, page 32
Small Wholemeal Honey Pitas, page 23, with the tops cut off
Shredded iceberg lettuce
Cashew-Sultana Chutney (recipe follows)

1.   Heat the oil in a frying pan. Add the turmeric, cumin, ginger, cardamom, and caraway seeds and cook over low heat until fragrant, 2 to 3 minutes; be careful not to burn the spices.

ABOUT CURRIES IN A PITA

While curries are generally served on a bed of rice to absorb the sauce, these recipes include just enough sauce to bind the meat and vegetables together. Anything more moist will soak through the pocket. If, however, the curries seem to need more liquid as they cook, add a bit more of the liquid called for in the recipe (such as orange juice or chicken stock)—just enough to keep them moist while retaining the binding quality. As an extra precaution, I have lined the pita pockets with shredded spinach or lettuce. For curry devotees, these pita stuffings laced with raitas and chutneys add new interest to a favourite dish. A note of warning, all the chutneys included here are *very* spicy—use them sparingly.

2. Add the bananas, carrots and salt and dried chilli flakes to the spices. Stir gently until thoroughly mixed, cover and sauté, stirring occasionally to keep the bananas and carrots from sticking, about 5 minutes.

3. Add the curry powder, orange juice, and lemon juice and stir gently. Be careful not to mash the bananas. Add the yogurt, cover and continue to simmer, stirring occasionally, until the curry is almost dry, 8 to 10 minutes. Taste to correct seasonings.

4. Line the pitas with the shredded lettuce. Spoon in the curry mixture and top with Cashew-Sultana Chutney.

Makes 4 to 6 servings.

Chashew-Sultana Chutney

150 g (5 oz) cashew nuts
2 hot green chillies, stemmed, seeded and chopped
30 ml (2 tbsp) chopped fresh parsley
45 ml (3 tbsp) fresh lemon juice
30 ml (2 tbsp) peeled and chopped fresh ginger
15 ml (1 tbsp) sultanas
Pinch of salt

Combine all the ingredients in a blender or food processor fitted with the metal blade. Process, until smooth, about 2 minutes. Add a little water, if necessary, to make a smooth paste. Refrigerate, covered, to chill. This fresh chutney is usually made to be used the same day but may be stored in the refrigerator for up to 1 week.

Makes bout 225 g (8 oz).

Indian-Inspired Buffet Lunch

Chilled Cucumber and Yogurt Soup with Garlic Pita Crisps
Lamb, Apple, and Almond Curry with Mint Chutney in Wheat-Germ Honey Pitas
Curry Condiments: Cucumber Raita, sliced pimientoes, shredded coconut, toasted almonds
Carrot, Orange and Radish Salad
Flaming Apricot Walnut Rolls
Iced Spiced Aniseed Tea
Lemonade with orange-blossom Water

OVEN-BAKED CHICKEN TANDOORI

With Cucumber Raita and Coconut-Apple Chutney

Recall the last time you had chicken tandoori in an Indian restaurant. It was moist, tangy, and a pinkish-red after having been marinated in a peppery yogurt sauce and slowly baked in a special oven. While we don't have these special ovens at home, this Oven-Baked Chicken Tandoori comes very close to the real thing. Marinate the chicken nuggets for 24 hours so the flavours of the yogurt, lemon, coriander, aniseed and dried chilli flakes have plenty of time to tenderize and season the meat, and use the remaining marinade to baste these morsels while they bake.

450 ml (¾ pint) yogurt, preferably homemade, page 32
30 ml (2 tbsp) fresh lemon juice
15 ml (1 tbsp) ground coriander
2.5 ml (½ tsp) crushed aniseeds
2.5 ml (½ tsp) crushed dried chilli flakes
Pinch of salt, or to taste
1.4 kg (3 lb) skinless, boneless chicken breasts, cut in 5 cm (2 inch) strips
75 ml (3 fl oz) vegetable oil
Small Basic Pitas, page 21, with the tops cut off
Shredded endive
Cucumber Raita (recipe follows)
Coconut-Apple Chutney (recipe follows)

1.   One day before serving, combine the yogurt, lemon juice, coriander, aniseed and dried chilli flakes and salt in a large bowl.

2.   Add the chicken strips and toss to coat thoroughly. Cover and marinate in the refrigerator, turning the pieces occasionally, overnight or preferably for 24 hours.

3.   Preheat the oven to 190°C (375°F) mark 5. Brush 45 ml (3 tbsp) of vege-table oil over the bottom of a roasting tin.

4.   Drain the chicken, reserving the marinade. Spread the chicken strips in the roasting tin and brush them with the remaining oil.

5.   Bake the chicken, turning and basting frequently with the reserved marinade, until tender, 30 to 40 minutes.

6.   Line the pitas with the shredded endive and lightly lace with the cucumber raita. Spoon in the chicken and top with a little coconut-apple chutney.

Makes 6 to 8 servings.

Cucumber Raita

2 cucumbers, peeled, seeded, and grated
Salt
450 ml (¾ pint) yogurt, preferably homemade, page 32
4 spring onions, finely chopped
1.25 ml (¼ tsp) ground cumin
Pinch of cayenne, optional

1. Place the shredded cucumbers in a colander set over a medium bowl. Sprinkle lightly with salt and toss to mix. Set aside for 30 minutes. Squeeze out the water. Pat the cucumbers dry on kitchen paper.

2. Combine the remaining ingredients in a medium bowl. Add the cucumber and stir gently to blend. Taste to correct seasonings. Refrigerate, covered, to chill.

Makes about 600 ml (1 pint).

Coconut-Apple Chutney

450 g (1 lb) (about 3) cooking apples, peeled and finely chopped
Pinch of salt
15 ml (1 tbsp) fresh lemon juice
225 g (8 oz) shredded coconut (see note)
3 medium onions, chopped
1 red or green pepper, cored, seeded, and chopped
15 ml (1 tbsp) peeled and chopped fresh ginger

1. Place the apples in a medium bowl. Sprinkle lightly with the salt and lemon juice and toss to coat. Set aside to drain, about 10 minutes.

2. Place the onions, pepper, and ginger in a blender or food processor fitted with the metal blade, and process until finely chopped.

3. Drain the apples. Add the onion mixture and the coconut. Toss to mix thoroughly. Refrigerate, covered, to chill. This fresh chutney is usually made to be used the same day but may be stored in the refrigerator for up to 3 days.

Makes about 700 g (1½ lb).

Note: If you use fresh coconut, shred it in a food processor and add 10 ml (2 tsp) sugar.

Working With Hot Chillies

Always wear rubber gloves when you are working with hot chillies. Never rub your hands against your eyes, nose, or mouth because the tissue in these areas is extremely sensitive to the chilli oils and fumes. After working with chillies, thoroughly wash both your hands and your gloves with soap and water.

CURRIED CRAB ROLLS
With Watercress Raita and Ginger-Sultana Chutney

Very similar to an Indian *Macchi Kofta* or a fish kebab, these crab rolls are fried to a crispy brown and served as appetizers or in pita pockets mounded with shredded lettuce and laced with Watercress Raita and Ginger-Sultana Chutney. Fresh coriander, curry powder, and cayenne promise a characteristic Indian flavour.

450 g (1 lb) shelled cooked crabmeat
3 eggs
45 ml (3 tbsp) mayonnaise
50 g (2 oz) fresh bread crumbs (about 2 slices of bread, crumbled)
225 g (8 oz) flour
15 ml (1 tbsp) finely chopped fresh coriander
5 ml (1 tsp) Madras curry powder or more, to taste
Cayenne, to taste
50 ml (2 fl oz) water
7.5 ml (1½ tsp) salt
2.5 ml (½ tsp) pepper
Vegetable oil for frying
Small Sesame Pitas, page 22, with the tops cut off
Shredded lettuce
Watercress Raita (recipe follows)
Ginger-Sultana Chutney (recipe follows)

1. Flake the crabmeat and place in a medium bowl. Beat 2 of the eggs until frothy and add to the crabmeat. Add the bread crumbs, 50 g (2 oz) of the flour, coriander, curry powder, and cayenne. Toss to combine thoroughly. Shape the crabmeat into 8 rolls; set aside.

2. Beat the remaining egg with the water in a small bowl. Combine the remaining flour, salt, and pepper in a pie plate. Dip the crabmeat rolls first in the beaten egg, then roll in the seasoned flour, coating well. Place on a greaseproof paper-lined plate and refrigerate, covered, until the rolls are firm and the coating is set, about 1 hour.

3. Pour the oil to a depth of 1 cm (½ inch) in a deep pan and heat until hot but not smoking. Fry the crab rolls, turning frequently, until golden brown, about 3 to 5 minutes. Drain on kitchen paper.

4. Line the pitas with the shredded lettuce and lace with the watercress raita. Put a crab roll inside each pocket and top with a little ginger-sultana chutney.

Makes 4 servings or 8 rolls.

Watercress Raita

450 ml (¾ pint) yogurt, preferably homemade, page 32
75 g (3 oz) finely chopped watercress
1 clove garlic, crushed
15 ml (1 tbsp) finely chopped green pepper
1.25 ml (¼ tsp) ground cumin
Salt, to taste
Cayenne, to taste

Combine all the ingredients in a

medium bowl. Stir them gently to blend. Taste to correct seasonings. Refrigerate, covered, to chill.

Makes about 900 ml (1 pint).

Ginger-Sultana Chutney

200 g (7 oz) peeled and chopped fresh ginger
1 hot green chilli, stemmed, seeded, and chopped
45 ml (3 tbsp) red wine vinegar
30 ml (2 tbsp) sultanas
Pinch of salt

Combine all the ingredients in a blender or food processor fitted with the metal blade. Process until smooth, about 2 minutes. Add a little water if necessary, to make a smooth paste. Refrigerate, covered, to chill. This fresh chutney is usually made to be used the same day but may be stored in the refrigerator for up to 1 week.

Makes about 225 g (8 oz).

LAMB, APPLE, AND ALMOND CURRY
With Mint Chutney

The last-minute addition of yogurt blends with the tomato paste to impart an added zest and create a pinkish sauce to coat this lamb, apple, and almond combination. Shredded spinach and mint chutney add a crowning touch!

30 ml (2 tbsp) vegetable oil or more, if necessary
900 g (2 lb) lamb leg or shoulder, cut in 2.5 cm (1 inch) cubes
1 large onion, chopped
2 cloves garlic, crushed
30 ml (2 tbsp) chopped fresh coriander
15 ml (1 tbsp) peeled and slivered fresh ginger
15 ml (1 tbsp) Madras curry powder
15 ml (1 tbsp) ground cumin
15 ml (1 tbsp) tomato paste

30 ml (2 tbsp) flour
Salt and freshly ground black pepper, to taste
350–450 ml (12–15 fl oz) hot chicken stock
2 medium cooking apples, peeled and chopped
50 g (2 oz) slivered almonds
175 ml (6 fl oz) yogurt, preferably homemade, page 32
Small Wheat-Germ Honey Pitas, page 24, with the tops cut off
Shredded fresh spinach
Mint Chutney (recipe follows)

1.   Heat the oil in a frying pan. Working in batches, add the lamb and sauté over medium-high heat, turning often, until well browned, about 15 minutes. Using a slotted spoon, remove the lamb as it is browned from the pan and place in a bowl.

2.   Reduce the heat to medium and add the onion and garlic to the pan and sauté, stirring frequently, about 5 minutes; add more oil, if necessary.

3.   Add the coriander, ginger, curry powder, cumin, tomato paste, flour, and salt and pepper, and cook over low heat, stirring constantly, until the spices become fragrant, about 1 minute; take care not to burn them.

4.   Return the lamb to the pan. Add the chicken stock beginning with 350 ml (12 fl oz) and increasing to 450 ml (15 fl oz), if necessary. (You need enough liquid to cook the meat yet not so much that it will drip through a pita pocket.) Cover and cook over low heat, stirring occasionally, until the lamb is tender, about 1 hour.

5.   Add the apples and almonds and cook until the apples are soft, about 5 minutes.

6.   Just before serving, stir in the yogurt. Heat thoroughly, stirring constantly.

7.   Line the pitas with the shredded spinach. Spoon in the lamb curry and top with mint chutney.

Makes 6 to 8 servings.

Mint Chutney

100 g (4 oz) fresh mint leaves
3 spring onions, chopped
1 hot green chilli, stemmed, seeded
*   and chopped*
45 ml (3 tbsp) fresh lemon juice
30 ml (2 tbsp) peeled and chopped
*   fresh ginger*
5 ml (1 tsp) sugar, or more, to taste
Pinch of salt

Combine all the ingredients in a blender or food processor fitted with the metal blade. Process until smooth, about 2 minutes. Add a little water, if necessary, to make a smooth paste. Refrigerate, covered, to chill. This fresh chutney is usually made to be used the same day but may be stored in the refrigerator for up to 1 week.

Makes about 100 g (4 oz).

PITA BURRITOS

I remember eating the best burritos ever at one of the many Mexican stands at Farmer's Market in Los Angeles. I thought then about making a Mediterranean-style burito by rolling "re-fried" chickpeas (instead of refried pinto beans) in a pita seasoned with spring onions and garlic and topped with melted cheese. If you've any leftover *Hummus Bi Tahini,* use that instead of the chickpeas.

6 Griddle-Baked Pitas, page 31
50 ml (2 fl oz) olive oil, or more, if
  necessary
150 g (5 oz) dried chickpeas, cooked
  and drained (see page 40) or 396 g
  (14 oz) can chickpeas, drained and
  rinsed
2 cloves garlic, crushed
Salt and freshly ground black
  pepper, to taste
45 ml (3 tbsp) finely chopped fresh
  coriander
5 spring onions, chopped
100 g (4 oz) Cheddar cheese, grated
Harissa (hot pepper sauce), page 108

1. Stack the pitas on a large square of kitchen foil. Seal and set aside.

2. Heat the oil in a frying pan. Add the beans and sauté over medium heat, mashing and stirring, to make a soft spreadable paste. Add more oil and some water, if necessary. Add the garlic, salt, and pepper, and stir until the mixture is softened and heated throughout. Taste to correct seasonings.

3. Preheat the oven to 150°C (300°F) mark 2. As the oven is preheating, place the foil-wrapped pitas in the oven, until warm and pliable, 5 to 8 minutes. Remove from the oven and unwrap. Lightly grease a large baking dish.

4. Spoon 90 ml (6 tbsp) of the seasoned bean mixture in the centre of each pita, spreading it to within 2.5 cm (1 inch) of the edge. Top the bean mixture with the coriander, onions and cheese, dividing it evenly among the 6 pitas. Roll the pitas closed and secure each with a toothpick. Place, folded-side down, in the prepared baking dish.

5. Bake in the oven until the cheese melts and the mixture is hot, 10 to 15 minutes.

6. Serve each burrito in a square of greaseproof paper and lace generously with *harissa.*

Makes 6 burritos.

CRISPY SESAME CHICKEN STRIPS

Friends will devour these tender oven-baked strips of sesame-seeded chicken stuffed in pitas and topped with Carrot, Orange and Radish Salad.

1 egg
50 ml (2 fl oz) water
100 g (4 oz) dry bread crumbs
30 ml (2 tbsp) flour
30 ml (2 tbsp) toasted sesame seeds
Salt and freshly ground black pepper, to taste
Pinch of cayenne, to taste
2 whole (about 700 g/1½ lb) skinless, boneless chicken breasts, pounded and cut into 7.5 cm (3 inch) strips
100 ml (4 fl oz) vegetable oil
Sesame Pitas, page 22, cut into halves
Shredded radicchio
Carrot, Orange and Radish Salad, page 94
Sesame-Honey Sauce, page 152

1.   Beat the egg and water in a small bowl. Combine the bread crumbs, flour, sesame seeds, salt, pepper, and cayenne on a plate. Dip the chicken strips first in the beaten egg, then roll in the bread crumbs, coating well. Place on a greaseproof paper-lined plate and refrigerate to set the coating, about 30 minutes to 1 hour.

2.   Pour the oil into a roasting tin and place in the oven. Preheat the oven to 190°C (375°F) mark 5. Remove the roasting tin from the oven. Add the chicken strips and coat them evenly with the oil.

3.   Place the chicken in the oven and bake, turning occasionally to brown all the sides, until golden-brown and tender, 35 to 40 minutes. Be careful not to overcook as the chicken will dry out.

4.   Line the pitas with the shredded lettuce and fill them with the chicken strips. Top with Carrot, Orange and Radish Salad and lace with Sesame-Honey Sauce.

Makes 4 to 6 servings.

PITA STROGANOFF

Mix sautéed onion, garlic, and mushrooms with lamb, season it delicately with sherry, then stir in tangy yogurt for a hearty Stroganoff.

40 g (1½ oz) butter
1 large onion, chopped
1 clove garlic, minced
225 g (8 oz) mushrooms, wiped clean with damp kitchen paper, and sliced
700 g (1½ lb) lean lamb, cut in thin 2.5 cm (1 inch) strips
175–225 ml (6–8 fl oz) water
50 ml (2 fl oz) dry sherry
Salt and freshly ground black pepper, to taste
15 ml (1 tbsp) flour
225 ml (8 fl oz) yogurt, preferably homemade, page 32
Small Wheat-Germ Honey Pitas, page 24, with the tops cut off
Shredded lettuce
Chopped tomatoes (garnish)
Chopped parsley (garnish)

1. Melt the butter in a frying pan. Add the onion, garlic, and mushrooms, and sauté over medium heat until all the water has evaporated from the mushrooms and the onions are soft but not brown, 5 minutes.

2. Stir in the lamb and cook, stirring occasionally, until the meat loses its pink colour, about 5 minutes.

3. Add the water, sherry, salt, and pepper. Stir and cover. Reduce the heat to low and continue cooking, stirring occasionally, until tender, about 45 minutes to 1 hour.

4. In a small bowl, blend the flour with the yogurt. Slowly stir it into the meat mixture. Continue cooking, stirring constantly, until the sauce is heated through and thickened. Taste to correct seasonings.

5. Line the pitas with the shredded lettuce and fill with the stroganoff. Top each with the chopped tomatoes and parsley.

Makes 4 to 6 servings.

THE PITA CROQUE MONSIEUR

Make a French sandwich by spreading the insides of a Basic Pita with Dijon mustard and filling it with thin slices of ham and cheese —Cheddar, Gruyère, or munster. Carefully dip it in a mixture of egg and milk (15 ml/1 tbsp milk to 1 egg) and sauté it in a blend of 15 g (½ oz) butter and 15 ml (1 tbsp) vegetable oil, as you would French Toast. Serve it with a light cheese sauce for extra zest.

MUSTARD STEAK AND BUCHERON

If you think the only way to cook flank steak is to braise it, I beg you to try it grilled. When we were first married, my husband introduced me to this way of cooking and slicing this normally less tender cut of beef. Its tenderness lies in the slicing. Smother it first with Dijon-style mustard and Worcestershire sauce, grill it to your favourite doneness—I like it medium-rare—then diagonally slice it paper-thin. Pile it in a pita topped with a mild goat cheese, chopped spring onions, and tomatoes. You've a memorable sandwich offering that calls for a mug of beer to top it off!

75 ml (3 fl oz) Dijon mustard
50 ml (2 tbsp) Worcestershire sauce
450 g (1 lb) flank steak
50 g (2 oz) butter, softened
Small Basic Pitas, page 21, with the tops cut off
Freshly ground black pepper
225 g (8 oz) Bucheron or similar soft goat cheese
Rocket (garnish)
Chopped spring onions (garnish)
Chopped tomatoes (garnish)
Salt and freshly ground black pepper, to taste

1. Blend the mustard and Worcestershire sauce in a small cup. Smother both sides of flank steak with the mustard mixture. Cover and marinate in the refrigerator, turning occasionally, 1 hour or more.

2. Butter the insides of the pita and wrap in clean, dry tea-towels to prevent them from drying out. Set aside.

3. Preheat the grill.

4. Sprinkle the steak on both sides with the freshly ground black pepper. Grill to medium-rare, about 5 minutes on each side.

5. Cut the steak on the diagonal into very thin slices and divide it and the Bucheron evenly among the buttered pitas. Garnish with the rocket, chopped onions, and tomatoes. Season with salt and pepper to taste.

Makes 4 servings.

Celebration Supper

Fried Lemon-Laced Cheese in Griddle-Baked Pitas
Piquant Pickled Turnips
Pita Charcuterie
Mustard Steak and Bucheron in Basic Pitas
Tomato and Onion Salad
Minted Potato Salad
Stuffed Dates in Pita wedges
Iced Beer
Hot Coffee

GINGERED TOFU AND VEGETABLE TOSS

The zippy flavour of ginger and the subtlety of tofu join forces to create these wonderful crispy-tender golden brown nuggets of goodness! Shredded Chinese cabbage and Coconut-Apple Chutney make great companions.

30 ml (2 tbsp) vegetable oil
4 spring onions, chopped
1 clove garlic, minced
Crushed, dried chilli flakes, to taste
100 g (4 oz) firm tofu, cut into 2.5 cm (1 inch) cubes
1 small cucumber, peeled, cut in half lengthwise, seeded and sliced
225 g (8 oz) bean sprouts
5 ml (1 tsp) peeled and slivered fresh ginger
225 g (8 oz) mange tout, trimmed
15 ml (1 tbsp) soy sauce, or more, to taste
Medium Wholemeal Sesame Pitas, page 24, cut into halves
Shredded Chinese cabbage
Coconut-Apple Chutney, page 135

1.   Heat the oil in a frying pan or wok. Add the spring onions and garlic and stir-fry over medium-high heat, about 1 minute. Stir in the dried chilli flakes and continue cooking to release the flavour, about 10 seconds.

2.   Add the tofu and stir-fry for 2 minutes. Add the cucumber, bean sprouts, and ginger and continue cooking until well coated and hot, about 1 to 2 minutes.

3.   Add the mange tout and soy sauce and stir-fry 1 minute longer. Taste to correct seasonings.

4.   Line the pitas with the shredded cabbage and fill with the tofu-vegetable toss. Add a dollop of coconut-apple chutney on top.

Makes 4 to 6 servings.

PEACEMAKER IN A POCKET

Peacemaker is the term given to a well-known New Orleans tradition. Years ago, errant husbands coming home late at night would bring hot, crispy oyster-filled loaves known as Les Mediatrices or mediators to appease their waiting wives. I've adapted the recipe to stuff the succulent oysters in pita pockets instead of hollowing out French loaves.

Flour, for coating
2 eggs
50 ml (2 fl oz) water
Dry bread crumbs
36 fresh or frozen oysters, thawed
50 g (2 oz) melted butter (15 g/½ oz per loaf)
4 medium Basic Pitas, page 21, cut into halves
Vegetable oil, for frying
Fresh lemon juice (garnish)

1. Place the flour on a large plate. Beat the eggs and water in a small bowl. Place the bread crumbs on a second plate. Drain the oysters, then coat them with flour, dip them in the beaten eggs, and roll in the bread crumbs, coating well. Place on a greaseproof paper-lined plate and refrigerate, covered, to set the coating, about 30 minutes to 1 hour.

2. Butter the inside of the pitas and stack on a large square of kitchen foil. Seal and set aside.

3. Preheat the oven to 150°C (300°F) mark 2.

4. Pour the oil to a depth of 1 cm (½ inch) in a deep pan and heat until hot but not smoking. Working in batches, add the oysters a few at a time, and fry them over medium-high heat until golden, about 3 to 4 minutes; do not crowd the pan. Drain the oysters on kitchen paper.

5. Warm the pitas in the oven for 2 to 3 minutes. Be careful that they do not get too crisp.

6. Fill the warm pita halves with hot oysters. Drizzle with lemon juice and serve immediately.

Makes 4 servings.

Orangeade with Orange-Blossom Water

A first cousin to lemonade, serve this hot or cold.

350 ml (12 oz) fresh orange juice
50 ml (2 fl oz) fresh lemon juice
50 ml (2 fl oz) iced water
2.5–5 ml (½–1 tsp) orange-blossom water, to taste
Sugar, to taste
Ice
Orange slices (garnish)
Fresh basil leaves (garnish)

Combine the orange juice, lemon juice, ice water, orange-blossom water, and sugar in a jug. Blend well. Pour into ice-filled glasses. Garnish with orange slices and basil leaves.

Makes 2 to 3 servings

ORANGE-GINGERED CHICKEN

Orange and ginger combine wonderfully with chicken in this tasty stir-fry with vegetables all piled into Poppy-Seed Pitas.

100 ml (4 fl oz) fresh orange juice
30 ml (2 tbsp) soy sauce
5 ml (1 tsp) cornflour
2.5 ml (½ tsp) ground ginger
40 g (1½ oz) fresh ginger, peeled and cut into julienne strips
2.5 ml (½ tsp) dried chilli flakes
2 cloves garlic, crushed
450 g (1 lb) skinless, boneless chicken breasts, cut into julienne strips
30 ml (2 tbsp) vegetable oil
275 g (10 oz) fresh or frozen mange tout, trimmed and cut into strips
1 small red pepper, cored, seeded, and cut into bite-sized pieces
225 g (8 oz) mushrooms, wiped clean with damp kitchen paper, and sliced
Medium Poppy-Seed Pitas, page 22, cut into halves
225 g (8 oz) shredded Chinese cabbage
Chopped fresh coriander (garnish)

1. Combine the orange juice, soy sauce, cornflour, ground and fresh ginger, dried chilli flakes and garlic in a large bowl. Add the chicken and stir to coat. Cover and marinate in the refrigerator, turning the pieces occasionally, about 2 hours.

2. Drain the chicken and reserve the marinade. Heat the oil in a frying pan or wok. Add the chicken and stir-fry over medium-high heat until cooked, about 5 to 8 minutes. Add the mange tout, pepper, and mushrooms, and continue cooking, tossing frequently until the vegetables are crisp-tender, about 3 to 5 minutes. Add the reserved marinade and cook until the liquid has been reduced by half.

3. Line the pitas with the shredded cabbage, fill with the chicken-vegetable mixture, and top with the coriander.

Makes 4 to 6 servings.

PITA SWEETS

Pitas work most creatively when it comes to desserts. Turn them into pancakes, puffs, rolls, puddings, and crisps to be combined with fresh and dried fruits, nuts, soft cheeses, and many other classic ingredients of the Middle East which are popular today as healthy alternatives to calorie-laden desserts and rich chocolate cakes.

Pita is also a handy accompaniment to simple sweets such as Stuffed Dates, Pressed Apricot Rolls, and Halvah, and Sweet Pita Crisps are delicious with light flavourful dips such as Sesame and Carob Sauce. Whatever your choices from the pita variations on old-fashioned American favourites such as Spiced Apple Pudding with Vanilla Sauce to exotic Flaming Apricot Walnut Rolls, guests will compliment your ingenuity and ask for more.

PITA CHEESE CRÊPES
With Orange-Blossom Syrup

Almost every country in the world has a cheese-filled pastry and the Middle East is no exception. In fact, there are numerous varieties— some rolled in phyllo pastry, others in a pancake-like crêpe and still others in a wheat- or barley-topped confection, but the common denominator is that they are all laced with a wonderful syrup of sugar, lemon juice, and orange-blossom water. This recipe uses the paper-thin but chewy Griddle-Baked Pitas to wrap around sweetened Yogurt Cheese or ricotta cheese. An exotic way to end a dinner for special guests. Serve them with Turkish coffee.

350 g (12 oz) unsalted Yogurt Cheese, page 33, or ricotta cheese
30 ml (2 tbsp) sugar, or more to taste
15 ml (1 tbsp) grated lemon rind
6 Griddle-baked Pitas 18–20.5 cm (7–8 inches), page 31
25 g (1 oz) melted butter
350 ml (12 fl oz) Orange-Blossom, Syrup (recipe follows)

1.   Blend the yogurt cheese or ricotta with the sugar and grated lemon rind until smooth. Taste to correct seasonings. Set aside.

2.   Cut the pitas in half and square the edges to make 12 strips, 8.5–10 cm (3½–4 inches) wide.

3.   Preheat the oven to 180°C (350°F) mark 4. Lightly grease a large shallow baking dish.

4.   Divide the cheese mixture equally between the pita strips, spreading it to the edges. Roll the strips lengthwise and place, seam-side down, in the baking dish. Brush with the melted butter.

5.   Bake, until heated through, 15 to 20 minutes. Serve warm, topped with orange-blossom syrup.

Makes 12 crêpes or 6 servings.

Orange-Blossom Syrup

550 g (1¼ lb) sugar
350 ml (12 fl oz) water
15 ml (1 tbsp) fresh lemon juice
5 ml (1 tsp) orange-blossom water, or more, to taste

1.   Combine the sugar, water, and lemon juice in a medium saucepan. Bring to a boil over high heat, stirring frequently. Reduce the heat to low and cook, uncovered, until the syrup falls in two or three heavy drops from a spoon, or registers 100°C (212°F) on a sugar thermometer.

2.   Immediately remove from the heat and let cool. Stir in the orange-blossom water. Serve the syrup at room temperature.

Makes about 450 g (1 lb).

Variations *Rose Water Syrup:* Substitute 2.5 ml (½ tsp) rose water, or more, if desired, for the orange-blossom water.

Cinnamon Syrup: Add 1 cinnamon stick to the syrup after reducing the heat to low. Omit the orange-blossom water.

FLAMING APRICOT-WALNUT ROLLS

The tangy flavour of apricots is enhanced immeasurably when these elegant little rolls are laced with Cognac and flambéed. They made a nice change of pace from Crêpes Suzettes.

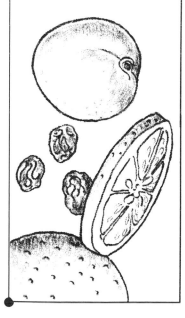

225 g (8 oz) dried apricots
100 g (4 oz) sugar
15 ml (1 tbsp) fresh lemon juice
2.5 ml (½ tsp) grated orange rind, or
    more to taste
50 g (2 oz) chopped walnuts
6 Griddle-baked Pitas 18–20.5 cm
    (7–8 inches), page 31
350 g (12 oz) unsalted Yogurt
    Cheese, page 33
25 g (1 oz) melted butter
350 ml (12 fl oz) Rose Water Syrup,
    page 148
60 ml (4 tbsp) Cognac

1.   One day before serving, put the apricots in a medium bowl and cover with cold water. Let them soak overnight. Drain, reserving the water and cut the apricots into small pieces.

2.   Place the reserved apricot water in a saucepan. Add the sugar and lemon juice and bring to a boil. Boil for 5 minutes. Add the apricots, reduce the heat, and simmer, stirring frequently, until the liquid has thickened, 30 to 45 minutes. Add the orange rind and nuts and cook for another 5 minutes. Remove from the heat and let cool.

3.   Cut the pitas in half and square the edges to make 12 strips, 8.5–10 cm (3–4 inches) wide.

4.   Preheat the oven to 180°C (350°F) mark 4. Lightly grease a shallow baking dish.

5.   Divide the yogurt cheese equally between the pita strips, spreading it to the edges. Spread a layer of the glazed apricots over the cheese. Tightly roll the strips lengthwise and secure them with cocktail sticks. Place, seam-side down, in the baking dish. Brush with the melted butter.

6.   Bake until heated through, 15 to 20 minutes. Transfer the warm apricot rolls to a flambé pan and pour the Rose Water Syrup over them.

7.   Just before serving, heat the Cognac in a small saucepan over medium heat and pour it immediately over the rolls. Carefully ignite the Cognac and let the flames go out. Serve the rolls with a generous measure of the Cognac-laced syrup, about 60 ml (4 tbsp) per serving.

Makes 12 rolls or 6 servings.

SPICED GLAZED FIGS WITH HAZELNUTS

A little of these spicy figs with a toasted pita crisp is heavenly with a small cup of black coffee. Or serve them as a confection for a lazy weekend brunch.

450 g (1 lb) dried figs, chopped
Fresh orange juice, to cover (about
*   600 ml/1 pint)*
100 g (4 oz) sugar
Pinch of nutmeg
Pinch of ginger
1.25 ml (¼ tsp) ground cinnamon
100 g (4 oz) chopped hazelnuts
15 ml (1 tbsp) lemon juice
Sweet Sesame Pita Crisps, page 28

1. Place the figs in a medium saucepan. Add the orange juice just to cover and let soak for about 30 minutes.

2. Cook over medium heat for 30 minutes. Add the sugar, nutmeg, ginger, and cinnamon. Reduce the heat and continue cooking until the figs are glazed and mixture is slightly thickened, about 15 to 20 minutes.

3. Remove from the heat and add the hazelnuts and lemon juice. Serve warm or cold with sweet sesame pita crisps.

Makes about 6 servings.

Variation *Glazed Apricots with Walnuts:* Substitute dried apricots for the figs; cook as above, omitting spices.

Tip: You may stew and glaze whole figs and apricots instead of chopping them, if desired.

STUFFED DATES IN PITA WEDGES

Stuffed dates in pita wedges are excellent served with wine and cheese or as a light dessert. Make a batch and give them to a special friend, with a package of pita, of course. Pit large dates or use pitted dates. Slit them enough to insert walnut pieces, pecan halves, or blanched salted almonds. Or, stuff them with unsalted Yogurt Cheese, page 33. Press the edges of the dates together to anchor the stuffing and shake the dates in a paper bag filled with a mixture of brown sugar and cinnamon. Serve them inside Basic Pita wedges.

TURKISH COFFEE
(Kahwe Turki)

K*ahwe*, meaning coffee, plays an important role in Middle-Eastern life. An unsweetened version is always served during a sad occasion while a sweet blend is enjoyed at celebrations and other happy times. Many a business deal has also been sealed over a foamy cup of coffee. The foaminess is the secret to a good cup of Turkish coffee. Methodically follow the steps outlined below and you will make a perfect pot every time.

6 small cups cold water
30 ml (6 heaped tsp) ground Turkish Coffee
Sugar, to taste (optional)

Pour the water into a saucepan or tapered, long-handled brass or porcelain Turkish coffee pot. Bring to a boil and add sugar, if desired. Gradually add the coffee, stirring constantly, until it returns to a boil and becomes foamy. Remove from the heat and let the froth recede in the coffee pot. Return to the heat and bring the coffee back to a boil, stirring occasionally to keep the coffee foamy. Repeat this procedure once more. Spoon a portion of the foam into each small cup and pour in the coffee. The foam will rise to the top.

Makes about 6 small servings.

Variations *Cardamom Coffee:*   Add 2 to 3 split cardamom pods to the coffee before you add it to the water.

Spiced Coffee: Add 5 ml (1 tsp) of ground cinnamon or ginger to the coffee before you add it to the water.

BAKED RUBY QUINCE WITH WALNUTS

I remember mother serving juicy chunks of preserved sweet quince topped with walnuts—they were always so good but ever too sweet. This recipe brings to mind those ruby red preserves—the quince turn a reddish colour as they cook—without all that sugar and calorie-laden guilt! Try it served with crisp pita wedges for your next Sunday brunch or lazy weekend breakfast. According to legend, the early Greeks and Romans considered the quince sacred to the Goddess of Love. If you gave a quince to the one you love it was tantamount to an engagement symbol.

4 ripe, bright-yellow quince, peeled, cored, and cut in quarters
100 g (4 oz) sugar
450 ml (¾ pint) apple juice
15 ml (1 tbsp) fresh lemon juice
5 ml (1 tsp) rose water (optional)
Chopped walnuts
Yogurt, preferably homemade, page 32
Cinnamon Pita Crisps, page 28

1. Preheat the oven to 150°C (300°F) mark 2.

2. Place the quince quarters in a baking dish. Sprinkle with the sugar and add the apple juice. It should come to depth of 1 cm (½ inch) in the baking dish (use more or less as needed).

3. Bake, basting occasionally with the syrup, until tender, glazed and reddish in colour, 2 hours. Remove from the oven and add the lemon juice and rose water, if desired. Cool to room temperature.

4. Serve topped with chopped walnuts and a dollop of yogurt, and accompanied by cinnamon pita crisps.

Makes 4 servings.

Sweet Pita Crisps With Dipping Sauces

The best desserts are sometimes those that require very little work. This one fits the bill. Try it for a sweet ending to a casual weekend supper. Prepare 2 bowls each with 100 ml (4 fl oz) Tahini (sesame seed paste), page 41. Stir in 100 ml (4 fl oz) honey to the first bowl and 100 ml (4 fl oz) golden syrup to the second bowl to make each sauce. Add a little water if you prefer a thinner sauce. Serve with Sweet Sesame Pita Crisps, page 28, surrounded by apple and pear slices which are also good dipped in the sauces.

SPICED APPLE PITA PUDDING

With Vanilla Sauce

This old-fashioned bread pudding topped with apples is a great way to use up the tops left over from pitas you have filled.

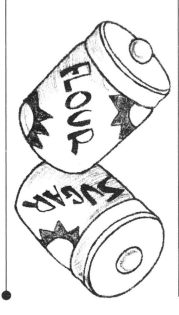

75 g (3 oz) raisins
40 g (1½ oz) butter
250 g (9 oz) pita cubes, cut in 4 cm (1½ inch) pieces
3 eggs
350 ml (12 fl oz) milk
100 ml (4 fl oz) double cream
125 g (5 oz) sugar
2.5 ml (½ tsp) grated orange rind
2.5 ml (½ tsp) ground cinnamon
1 large red eating apple, peeled, cored, and cut into 1 cm (½ inch) wedges
350–450 ml (12–15 fl oz) Vanilla Sauce (recipe follows)

1. Soak the raisins in boiling water until they are plumped, about 10 to 15 minutes. Drain thoroughly and dry with kitchen paper.

2. Melt the butter in a frying pan. Add the pita cubes and sauté over medium heat, tossing lightly, until well coated and just beginning to brown, about 5 minutes. Put the bread cubes and any remaining butter into a lightly buttered 23×23 cm (9×9 inch) baking dish. Add the raisins to the bread cubes and mix together.

3. Combine the eggs, milk, cream, 100 g (4 oz) of the sugar, and the orange rind in a medium bowl and beat together thoroughly. Pour over the bread cubes and raisin mixture, making certain the bread is thoroughly immersed. Refrigerate, covered with plastic wrap, for 1 hour.

4. Preheat the oven to 180°C (350°F) mark 4.

5. Combine the remaining sugar with the cinnamon. Arrange the apple wedges on top of the pudding and sprinkle with the cinnamon-sugar mixture.

6. Place the baking dish in a large roasting tin. Add enough hot water to come ⅔ of the way up the sides of the tin. Bake in the centre of the oven, until a thin-bladed knife inserted 2.5 cm (1 inch) from the edge comes out clean, 40 to 45 minutes. Remove from the oven and let cool to room temperature.

Makes 6 to 8 servings.

Vanilla Sauce

50 g (2 oz) sugar
22 ml (1½ tbsp) cornflour
1.25 ml (¼ tsp) salt
400 ml (14 fl oz) boiling water
*40 g (1½ oz) butter, cut into small
   pieces*
10 ml (2 tsp) vanilla essence

1.   Combine the sugar, cornflour and salt in a medium saucepan. Stir in the boiling water and cook over medium heat, stirring constantly, until thickened and clear, about 6 to 8 minutes. Simmer for an additional 3 minutes to cook the cornflour.

2.   Remove from the heat and add the butter and vanilla extract. Stir to blend. When the butter has melted, serve warm over the pudding.

Makes about 450 ml (¾ pint).

Pita Apple Crisps

Turn little pita loaves into a handy crust for a quick Apple Crisp, a favourite among children and adults alike.

Slit small pitas into individual rounds, spread them with softened butter, and top with a hefty dollop of apple sauce seasoned with sugar and cinnamon. Place them on a greased baking sheet and bake in a preheated 180°C (350°F) mark 4 oven until they are warm and heated through, about 10 to 12 minutes.

They are heavenly served warm and topped with a scoop of vanilla ice cream.

PITA AND HALVAH

Halvah is a confection made of ground sesame seeds and honey, sugar, or glucose, bound together with egg white. Originally a Turkish specialty, halvah is now widely found throughout the Middle East. It comes plain, marbled, chocolate-coated, or with pistachios and may be purchased in the refrigerated sections of well-stocked supermarkets, health food stores, specialist or ethnic food shops. It is traditionally eaten with pita bread, which balances its cloyingly sweet taste.

Cut small pitas into halves or triangles and insert slices of halvah. Serve these with apple slices, grapes, or melon balls, and offer strong, sweet Turkish coffee to make a delightful ending to simple meal.

PISTACHIO AND BANANA TOFFEE ROLLS

With Grand Marnier Syrup and Crème Fraîche

These fruit and nut rolls laced with warm Grand Marnier Syrup and Crème Fraîche make an unusual dessert for a special occasion.

225 g (8 oz) coarsely chopped
   pistachio nuts
50 g (2 oz) light brown sugar
25 g (1 oz) butter, softened
6 Griddle-Baked Pitas 18–20.5 cm
   (7–8 inches), page 31
3 medium bananas, peeled and cut
   in half (each half should be about
   6.5–7.5 cm/2½–3 inches long)
25 g (1 oz) butter, melted
350 ml (12 fl oz) Grand Marnier
   Syrup, (recipe follows)
Crème Fraîche (recipe follows)

1. Combine the nuts, sugar, and softened butter in a medium bowl. Set aside.

2. Cut the pitas in half and square the edges to make 12 strips, 8.5–10 cm (3½–4 inches) wide.

3. Preheat the oven to 180°C (350°F) mark 4. Lightly grease a shallow baking dish.

4. Divide the nut mixture equally between the pita strips, spreading it to the edges. Top each strip with a banana half. Tightly roll the strips lengthwise and secure them with cocktail sticks. Place, seamside down, in the baking dish. Brush with the melted butter.

5. Bake until heated through, about 15 to 20 minutes. Serve warm drizzled with the Grand Marnier Syrup, about 60 ml (4 tbsp) per serving. Top with a dollop of crème fraîche.

Makes 6 servings.

Grand Marnier Syrup

400 g (14 oz) sugar
450 ml (¾ pint) water
15 ml (1 tbsp) fresh lemon juice
30 ml (2 tbsp) Grand Marnier

1. Combine the sugar, water, and lemon juice in a medium saucepan. Bring to a boil over high heat, stirring frequently. Reduce the heat to low and cook, uncovered, until the syrup falls in two or three heavy drops from a spoon, or registers 100°C (212°F) on a sugar thermometer.

2. Immediately remove from the heat and let cool. Stir in the Grand Marnier. Serve the syrup at room temperature.

Makes 450 ml (¾ pint).

Crème Fraîche

100 ml (4 fl oz) double cream
100 ml (4 fl oz) soured cream

1. One day before serving, whisk together the double cream and soured cream in a medium bowl. Cover and set aside in a warm place until thickened, 8 hours to overnight.

2. Refrigerate, covered to chill for 4 to 6 hours to develop its characteristic tart flavour.

Makes about 225 ml (8 fl oz).

PRESSED APRICOT ROLLS

As children we used to call this sweet-like confection made from puréed apricots "shoe leather" because it looked like the leather which was sold by the yard before it was made into shoes. When we purchased it we literally bought it by the yard and tore it into bite-sized pieces to eat. It can be made without too much fuss at home.

Mince 900 g (2 lb) dried apricots and 450 g (1 lb) dried peaches twice in a mincer using the finest cutting wheel or process them in a food processor fitted with the metal blade until they are puréed or finely minced. Sprinkle a cutting board heavily with icing sugar and knead the apricot-peach mixture until it is smooth, about 8 to 10 minutes, then pat and roll it to a thickness of 0.3 cm (⅛ inch). Cut it into 5 cm (2 inch) strips and roll each into a tight little roll. Set them overnight in an uncovered dish or pan to dry. Store in an airtight container for up to 3 weeks. Makes about 1.4 kg (3 lb).

These dainty rolls are a favourite lunch-box treat for children, or a convenient dessert served with Sesame pita toast and a piquant cheese such as Roquefort.

GLAZED PITA PUFFS
(Awamat)

These syrup-bathed doughnut puffs are favourite sweetmeats all over Middle Eastern and Mediterranean countries. Called awamat in Arabic, zeppoli in Italy, diples in Greece, and doughnuts in Europe, these deep-fried dollops of dough are a little bite of heaven!

½ recipe Basic Pita dough, page 21, prepared up to step 2
Vegetable oil, for frying
350–450 ml (12–15 fl oz) Orange-Blossom Syrup, page 148

1. Place the dough in a large greased bowl and turn the dough over to bring the greased side up. Cover the bowl with a clean dry tea-towel and let the dough rise in a warm draught-free area until it is light and spongy, about 1 to 1½ hours.

2. Pinch off pieces of the dough about 2.5–4 cm (1–1½ inches) in diameter. Shape into balls, cover with a clean dry tea-towel and let them rise for another 30 minutes.

3. Pour the oil to a depth of 4 cm (1½ inches) in a deep pan and heat until hot but not smoking. Working in batches of 5 or 6 at a time, fry the pieces until they are golden-brown on all sides, about 1 minute. Using a slotted spoon, remove them and drain on kitchen paper.

4. Dip the warm fritters into the cold syrup and place them on a serving platter. Drizzle more syrup over the puffs before serving.

Makes about 36.

Variations *Sugared Puffs:* Instead of dipping the puffs into the syrup, dust them lightly with icing sugar.

MINT TEA
(Shī)

S *hī*, pronounced similarly all over the Middle East, even if spelled differently, means tea. This minty version is refreshing, especially when served with Glazed Pita Puffs, page 157, or Pita Apple Crisps, page 154. In the summer, pour the tea over ice and garnish it with a mint sprig and a slice of orange for a thirst-quenching cooler.

900 ml (1½ pints) water
15 ml (3 tsp) green China tea, such as Gunpowder
Sugar or honey, to taste
25 g (1 oz) fresh mint sprigs, chopped
Additional fresh mint sprigs (garnish)

Pour the water into a large saucepan and bring to a boil. Stir in the tea and sugar or honey. Place the mint sprigs in a warmed teapot and pour in the sweetened tea. Cover and let steep for 5 to 7 minutes. Strain into tea cups or glasses. Top each with a mint sprig.

Makes about 4 to 6 servings.

GLOSSARY
AND
INDEX

GLOSSARY

What follows is an explanation of various recipe ingredients that may be unfamiliar.

Broad Beans

A member of the pulse family, broad beans have broad pods and large flat seeds. They are used in making Egyptian Bean Croquettes, page 107, or combined with chickpeas to make *Falafel*, page 107. Kidney or similar beans make excellent substitutes. Broad beans are available in health food stores and supermarkets.

Bulgur

A grain product made by parboiling and drying whole-wheat kernels and crushing them into various sizes from fine to coarse grades. It is not to be confused with cracked wheat or crushed wheat. Bulgur is used for making *Kibbeh*, page 51, and *Tabbouleh*, page 98. It is available in health food stores and ethnic grocers.

There seems to be a wide variety of opinion among food experts and cookbook writers on how to prepare bulgur. Some feel it should be soaked for long periods in hot water while others suggest cooking it first. None of this is necessary, in my opinion, as such methods will make the bulgur too soft and mushy. Simply rinse the bulgur and place it in a bowl. Cover with cool tap water and let soak until it is tender to the bite, about 20 to 30 minutes. Drain thoroughly and squeeze out any excess water. Fluff the bulgur to separate the grains. Now it's ready to use.

Carob

A powder made from the brown fruit or pod of the carob or locust tree (often called St. John's bread), found along the shores of the Mediterranean. It resembles unsweetened cocoa powder both in texture and taste and can act as a substitute for those who are allergic to chocolate. It is used to flavour puddings and sweets. Carob powder is available in most health food stores.

Chickpeas

Round, marble-like beans used for making *Hummus Bi Tahini*, page 40, or *Falafel*, page 107.

Chickpeas are available in most supermarkets in both their canned and dried form. The canned chickpeas need only be drained to be ready to use. To prepare dried chickpeas, put 150 g (5 oz) dried chickpeas in a medium bowl, cover with water to the top of the bowl, and soak overnight. Drain, put in a saucepan, and cover with fresh water. Cover and bring to a boil, then reduce the heat and cook until soft, about 1 hour. Drain and cool. This makes about 350 g (12 oz) cooked chickpeas.

Clarified Butter

Butter which is melted and skimmed of all its sediment, impurities, and dairy solids. In the case of melted salted butter, the salt is also removed. The remaining liquid is a clear transparent yellow. When cooled, clarified butter solidifies and becomes opaque. Because it develops its own built-in preservative as it is heated, clarified butter does not need to be refrigerated; however, for long-term storage it is best kept under refrigeration. See page 56 for information on how to clarify butter.

Coriander Leaves

The coriander plant is an annual herb, related to the parsley family. It has a pungent, penetrating aroma and taste and is used in many Middle Eastern, Mediterranean, and Oriental dishes. Coriander is available in most greengrocers.

Coriander Seeds

The coriander plant bears seed-like fruit with a pleasing aromatic taste. Morocco supplies most of the world's crop. The tiny seeds must be thoroughly dried before their characteristic flavour and fragrance develop. When crushed or ground, their aroma and flavour is like a combination of aniseed, cumin, and orange peel. Coriander is available in the spice section of supermarkets as both ground and whole seeds. It is used to season many savoury dishes.

Cumin

A spice gathered from a low-growing plant native to the Mediterranean, cumin is probably most familiar as the major ingredient in curry and chilli powders. It is also used as a pungent seasoning in dips, salad and sandwich mixtures, dressings, sauces, and rice dishes. It is available in the spice section of supermarkets both as a dusty gold powder and as whole seeds.

Curry Powder

A blend of ground spices including turmeric, fenugreek, cumin, coriander, and cayenne that is commonly used in Indian cuisine. Some blends such as Madras curry powder are more assertive and pungent than others. Madras curry powder is available in the imported food and/or the spice section of most supermarkets.

Feta Cheese

A crumbly white cheese usually made of sheep's milk and ripened in a brine solution. There are mild, medium, and sharp feta cheeses, depending on how long they have been aged prior to being immersed in the brine. Feta is generally sold directly from the brine solution, which may be made from milk and salt or water and salt. Feta is available in cheese shops, Greek grocers, and some supermarkets.

Figs

There are some 800 varieties of figs, varying in shape and colour. The fig has been cultivated since the earliest civilization and was regarded as a symbol of peace and plenty by the early Hebrews. There are green, white, purple or black varieties of figs. They have juicy flesh full of tiny edible seeds. Most figs have thin skins which are edible. Figs are available fresh or dried. Fresh fruit should be soft to the touch and have skins with a distinct bloom. Dried figs are available in supermarkets and health food stores.

Harissa

A pungent paste made from hot chillies and used as a condiment, dipping sauce, or as a dressing for pita sandwiches. See page 108 for the recipe. Similar hot sauces are available in ethnic grocers.

Jiban

A firm, textured, fresh white cheese made from whole milk and blended with yogurt and fresh lemon juice to form a curd. The curd is removed from the whey, pressed into patties, salted, and stored in some of the reserved whey, or seasoned, tied into a cheesecloth bag, and marinated in olive oil. See page 36 for the recipe.

Labani (yogurt cheese)

A soft cheese similar in texture to softened cream cheese but with a more tangy flavour. It is made from draining the water or whey from yogurt and is used as a spread or as an ingredient in appetizers and main dishes. See page 33 for the recipe.

Olive oil

A mono-unsaturated oil made from the fruit of the olive tree. A good extra virgin olive oil (made from the first pressing) is traditionally used in Middle Eastern salad and dip recipes because it imparts a characteristically savoury flavour and aroma. Use olive oil also for frying or sautéeing when it is specifically recommended as it will impart a classic flavour to the finished dish. For all other frying and sautéeing, use a pure vegetable oil.

Olives

Of the many varieties of black olives available, my favourites are Alfonse and Calamata. Alfonse olives are very large, purplish-black Greek olives with a soft texture and assertive flavour. Calamata olives are small, oval-shaped, almost-black Greek olives with a firm texture and assertive flavour. Olives are available in ethnic grocers, specialist shops and food shops, and most supermarkets. See page 82 for information on how to marinate olives.

Orange-blossom water

A distilled liquid made from orange blossoms and used to flavour beverages, syrups, pastries, and desserts. Rose water, made from rose petals, is a similar liquid and an excellent alternative. Both orange-blossom water and rose water are available in ethnic grocers, some supermarkets and chemists.

Pine nuts

Small white or cream-coloured nuts from the inside of the hard outer casing of the pine cone. They are used for main dishes, stuffings, and salads, or, when toasted, as a garnish or topping. They are available in specialist food shops and some supermarkets. To toast pine nuts on top of the cooker spread them in a well-seasoned cast-iron pan or pan with non-stick surface. Cook over medium heat, shaking frequently, until the pine nuts turn golden-brown and smell fragrant, about 5 to 8 minutes. To toast pine nuts in the oven, preheat the oven to 180°C (350°F) mark 4. Spread the pine nuts on a baking tray and bake, shaking frequently until golden-brown and fragrant, about 8 to 10 minutes.

Prickly pear

The leaves of the prickly pear cactus plant family (genus Opuntia), with the prickles removed. Prickly pears are parboiled, cooled, sliced or shredded, and used as a vegetable or as an ingredient in salads and appetizers.

Rose Water	See Orange-Blossom Water.	
Sesame seeds	Small cream-coloured seeds from a tropical and sub-tropical herbaceous plant, sesame seeds are used to sprinkle on top of breads, pastries, and sweets, as well as being the basis of sesame oil, Tahini (sesame seed paste), page 41, and the confection, halvah. They are available in supermarkets, health food stores, and ethnic grocers. Sesame seeds contain a great deal of oil. To prevent them from going rancid, store them in an airtight container in the refrigerator. Use within 3 months and always take a trial sniff before	including them in a recipe. If they have the aroma or flavour of old used oil, do not use them. To toast sesame seeds on top of the cooker spread them in a well-seasoned cast-iron pan or pan with a non-stick surface. Cook over medium heat, shaking frequently, until fragrant and light golden, about 5 minutes. To toast sesame seeds in the oven, preheat the oven to 180°C (350°F) mark 4. Spread the sesame seeds on a baking tray and bake, shaking frequently, until fragrant and light golden, about 8 minutes.
Sumac	A tart seasoning made from the dried ground seeds of a non-poisonous variety of the cashew plant. Sumac is used as a primary ingredient in *zahter* (see below), a	blend of herbs often used as a topping for pita. It is available in ethnic grocers. Lemon rind can be used as a substitute.
Tahini (sesame seed paste)	An oily paste made from ground sesame seeds and used to make sauces, dips, and dressings. Tahini is so common throughout the Mediterranean that no home is without it.	See page 41 for the recipe. Tahini is also available ready-made in health food stores, ethnic grocers, and many supermarkets.
Wheat Germ	The rich embryo of the wheat grain which is the fat-containing portion of the wheat kernel. It has a high concentration of nutrients—vitamins B	and E and minerals. It is available in health food stores. Add it to bread dough and casseroles and sprinkle it over cereal, soups, and desserts.

White Cheese

See *Jiban.*

Yogurt Cheese

See *Labani.*

Zahter

A blend of marjoram, thyme, toasted sesame seeds, and the tart, dried ground seeds of the sumac plant. It is used for seasoning breads and salads in Middle Eastern recipes. You can make an acceptable substitute by mixing 5 ml (1 tsp) each of toasted sesame seeds, dried marjoram, dried thyme, freshly grated lemon rind, and a pinch of salt. Makes about 7 g (¼ oz). Store like other spices, in a cool, dry place.

INDEX